KU-265-765

Grasses

A CONCISE GUIDE IN COLOUR

Grasses

by
Dr. Jaromír Šikula

Illustrated by
Vojtěch Štolfa

HAMLYN

LONDON • NEW YORK • SYDNEY • TORONTO

Translated by Olga Kuthanová
Designed and produced by Artia for
The Hamlyn Publishing Group Limited
London • New York • Sydney • Toronto
Astronaut House, Feltham, Middlesex, England
Copyright © 1978 Artia, Prague
All Rights Reserved. No part of this publication may be
reproduced or transmitted in any form or by any means,
electronic or mechanical, including photocopy, recording,
or any information storage and retrieval system, without
permission in writing from the copyright owner.

ISBN 0 600 34045 7

Printed in Czechoslovakia
3/02/31/51–01

CONTENTS

FOREWORD

Of all existing plants, grasses have played the most important role in the life of mankind, those of greatest value being the cereals — wheat, rice, maize, barley, rye, oats, millet and sorghum. They have, therefore, become the symbol of prosperity — indeed, the word 'cereal' is derived from Ceres, the name given by the Romans to the Greek goddess of agriculture. To this day cereals are the backbone of crop production just as cattle are the backbone of animal production.

Cereals were not, however, the only grasses that helped man to obtain food and nourishment. Also important were the meadow and pasture grasses. A natural meadow grassland, composed of many species of grasses and herbs, is a remarkable biological community that does not suffer from soil fatigue. Its fertility constantly increases and rich humus deposits are retained in the soil. This fact was put to use by our forefathers who observed the practice of leaving land fallow and in modern agriculture many countries recognize the advantages of grass–tillage to this day.

Years of breeding and selection have produced cereals and other plants which are highly productive. Cereals and their grains have become a particularly important source of food which, like animal fodder, can be easily stored for long periods without any loss in quality. So the yield of grasses and especially of cereals must continue to be regarded as a source of prosperity.

Grasses and grasslands occur naturally and are capable of thriving in the climate of the arctic, the desert or the mountains, in dry conditions or damp, marshland or water, in soil that is acid or basic, rich or poor in minerals, heavy or light, in shaded as well as in exposed localities, and even in places blighted by industrial pollution and toxic chemicals. This alone is reason enough for man to value grasses and to regard them not just as mere plants but as important helpmates.

Grasses generally form the low herb layer and are therefore an important element in keeping most expanses of land green, at least during the growing season. Whether annual, biennial or perennial, grasses play a significant role in preserving the natural fertility of the countryside. They prevent erosion by wind and water as well as the rapid penetration of rainfall, they form humus in the soil and promote the spread of soil micro-organisms and members of the soil fauna.

THE INGENIOUS STRUCTURE OF GRASSES

Grasses are extremely well-equipped plants that develop in perfect harmony with their external surroundings. In their shape and internal anatomy there is a constructional perfection that serves as an example and inspiration in solving various problems of modern building technology. Consider, for instance, a wheat or rye stem; its height, thinness, hollowness, flexibility, resilience and strength as well as resistance to unfavourable climatic conditions, cannot be rivalled even by the best quality steel, taking specific

Fig. 1 Section of the leaf of Red Fescue
a) folded leaf enclosed by the sheath   b) flat leaf

gravity as the basis of comparison. The stem is strong
and resilient because it contains several cylindrical
tubes, consisting of vascular bundles, closed at the
joints or nodes by solid tissue. The vascular bundles
consist of xylem and phloem with a sheath of thick-
walled cells impregnated with lignin. This woody
tissue causes stiffening of the stem, making it practically indigestible for animals but greatly increasing
the plant's strength, which is retained even after
the cells have died. The structure of the stem thus
resembles the structures used in the modern building
industry, the vascular bundles corresponding to the
steel bars and the sheath of thick-walled cells to
the concrete.

Just as remarkable is the structure of grass leaves,
which are adapted both in shape and function to

8

the external conditions of their environment. Drought-resistant grasses can roll the two halves of their long, thin blades so tightly that the leaves become threadlike. This peculiarity enables them to utilize even the water vapour passing through the stomata located on the inner side of the blade. The leaf structure of grasses with flat blades, however, is consistent with that of reinforced concrete structures. Through hairlike outgrowths called trichomes water vapour transpired from the leaves is retained. This helps to keep the grass alive even in extremely dry conditions. Even more remarkable is the grass fruit or seed which contains not only the embryo but also nutritive tissue (endosperm) serving as a food store for the germinating embryo as well as a source of precious energy in the form of carbohydrates and proteins for man and livestock. Due to the structure of the grain it can be easily stored in granaries and used for food when needed, or else as seed for sowing.

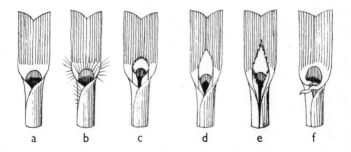

Fig. 2 Types of junction of leaf sheath and blade
a) without ligule   b) with fringe of hairs   c) collar-like, with toothed margin   d) pointed   e) irregularly toothed   f) membranous outgrowths called auricles

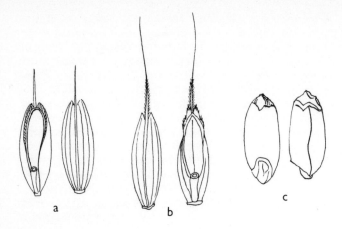

Fig. 3 Types of seed
a) with a short awn, enclosed by the lemma and palea
b) with a long awn, enclosed by the lemma and palea
c) naked, without lemma and palea

The external anatomy of grasses differs markedly from that of other plants and it is by the characteristics of the individual features that the various species can be determined.

The grass stem, or culm, is composed of several sections (internodes) and joints (nodes). The stem of most grasses is hollow; only in some species such as maize, millet and sugar cane is it solid. The nodes may be hairless or hairy. Arising at the nodes are the leaf sheaths, which may be open with free margins, for example fescues, or entire with joined margins, such as in bromes. At the point where the leaf blade emerges from the sheath there is a thin membranous outgrowth called the ligule which may be short, longish, collar-like, elongate, pointed, irregularly toothed or very long. Sometimes this may be reduced to a fringe of short hairs. On the margin opposite the ligule some grasses have so-called auricles, small outgrowths more or less clasping the stem, which vary in length and are often wavy.

Leaf blades also exhibit fairly marked morphological differences. Individual grasses differ in the arrangement of the leaves in the leaf bud (vernation). These may be coiled, resembling a spiral in cross-section, or else folded and resembling the letter V in cross-section. In some leaves transverse stripes or white longitudinal stripes can be seen when held up to the light. The undersurface of the blade is usually variously keeled. The blade may be hairless or hairy and may be a different colour on the upper and underside. It may also be ribbed. Some grasses have very sharp ribs extending mid-way through the blade or even almost to the lower epidermis. Viewing the blade in cross-section one can see the arrangement of the ribs, which may be regular or irregular, and also whether the ribs are blunt or angular and sharp. Some grasses have a line of colourless cells (bulliform cells) on either side of the mid-rib making it possible to fold the leaf lengthwise by bringing the two halves together. The tips of leaf blades also show marked differences. In the Smooth Meadow-grass they are hooded, splitting into two points when pressed flat between the fingers. In some grasses the blades are abruptly pointed whereas in others they taper gradually towards the apex. Important characteristics in the identification of grasses, especially when flowers are not present, are the number of vascular bundles and their position in the blade and the hairiness or roughness and shape of the cross-section of the blade.

The flowers and inflorescences of grasses differ

from the flowers of other plants. The basic unit, or flower, consists of two enclosing bracts termed the lemma and palea, two small narrow scales at the base of the seed called lodicules, an ovary with two feathery stigmas on short styles, and usually three stamens. Only certain species of grasses differ from this basic type. Rice has six stamens, bamboos also have a great-

Fig. 4 Types of inflorescences
a) contracted spike b) loose spike c) racemose panicle
d) spike-like panicle e) loose racemose panicle f) – g) panicles of grasses h) feathery branched spike

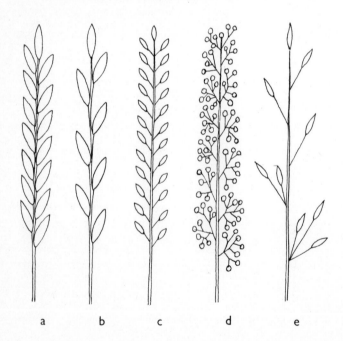

a   b   c   d   e

er number, and Sweet Vernal-grass has only two stamens. Matgrass has only a single feathery stigma. In many grasses the lemmas and glumes are furnished with slender bristle-like projections termed awns, which may be long or short, straight or bent. Oat-grasses, for example, have characteristic bent awns.

The flower is always enclosed in further scales called glumes. There are usually two of these but there may be more. The flower together with the glumes forms a one-flowered spikelet, for example in bents. A spikelet is said to be two-flowered if there are two flowers inside the glumes and multi-flowered if there are more. Again, these may be awned or awnless. The number of flowers in a spikelet and

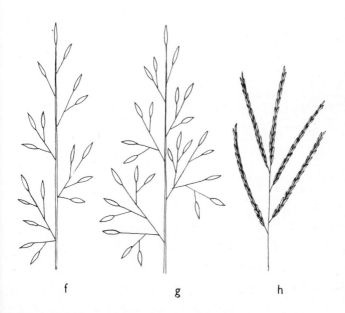

f   g   h

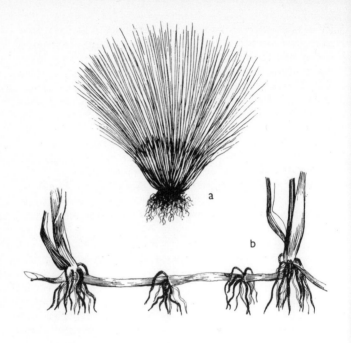

Fig. 5 Grasses
a) tufted   b) creeping

whether they are with or without awns are also important diagnostic characteristics at flowering time. The spikelets (one-flowered or multi-flowered) may be arranged in various ways, forming various types of flower heads or inflorescences. The inflorescence may be a raceme with the spikelets borne on short stalks on the main axis (a less common form typical of bromes), or it may be a panicle. Panicles may be open (Common Reed) or contracted (Purple

14

Moor-grass), erect (Smooth Meadow-grass) or pendulous (Millet), loose or dense, and may have long or short branches. They may also be very dense and spike-like (Timothy and Foxtail Grass). Another form of inflorescence is the true compound spike (wheat, rye and barley), and then there is the feathery-branched or finger-branched spike (male flower head of maize).

Another important point of identification is the way in which the grass spreads. Grasses may be tufted or creeping. Tufted grasses form dense bristly clusters, for example Matgrass; creeping grasses form loose continuous masses such as Smooth Meadow-grass. Grasses may spread by means of creeping stems over the surface of the soil (stolons) or by underground stems (rhizomes). Young shoots may grow through the bases of the enveloping leaf sheaths (extravaginal growth) or they may grow up within the enveloping leaf sheath (intravaginal growth). Shoots often have the power of developing roots. The shape of the roots and the depth to which they grow not only make it possible to identify many grasses but also to determine their resistance to drought and frost and whether they are annuals or perennials.

THE EVOLUTION AND GROWTH
OF GRASSES

All higher plants (with a body composed of root, stem and leaf) evolved about 350 million years ago when conditions on earth were conducive to evolutionary changes. Those that appeared at that time were the most primitive of the higher plants. Grasses, which are high up the evolutionary scale, appeared much later in the Cretaceous period, about 100 million years ago. Already widespread at that time were grasses that exist to this day, such as Common Reed and Giant Reed. Fossil remains in France have yielded information about the existence of certain species of bamboo in the Tertiary period, about eleven million years ago.

Grasses evolved from the ancestral types of dicotyledonous plants into monocotyledons to form a separate independent evolutionary branch in that group. Monocotyledonous plants differ in many ways from dicotyledons, mainly in the form and structure of the organs, in having an embryo containing only one seed leaf, and in producing adventitious roots in place of the dying primary root. Plants commonly known as 'sour grasses' resemble the true grasses but evolved along entirely different lines. These include rushes and sedges, which are close to plants of the lily family.

Modern scientists place grasses in a separate order Poales, formerly called Gramineae or Glumiflorae. This order contains only one family, the Poaceae. Today there are more than 600 genera and 8 000 – 10 000 species of grasses distributed throughout the world.

Beginning with germination, biological functions

in grasses have certain characteristic features and a characteristic sequence. Young plants spread and grow, flower, and then, following pollination and fertilization, produce seed. Perennial species, which have a life cycle of several years, repeat this process every growing season and some species may even flower several times in one year. Cocksfoot, when cut or grazed, will grow anew up to six times in succession during a single growing season but as a rule bears flowers only in May and occasionally in late summer. Annual grasses die after the seeds mature. This is typical of our cereal grasses and most annual weeds such as Annual Meadow-grass and Loose Silky-bent.

Grasses also have the remarkable ability of maintaining a water balance in their tissues. They are able to regulate the processes of transpiration and photosynthesis, adapt to changes in light and heat, and cover large areas in a very short time. Their growth and development have specific physiological laws and are governed by both external factors and the grasses' internal dynamics and rhythm. For example, if the tips of tall young shoots are removed by cutting, the plant's internal equilibrium is disrupted. In some species this results in stopping the flow of the plant hormone auxin, which flows from the top of the plant down toward the roots. This triggers a correlated reaction which activates the latent buds and the growth of new shoots. The differing powers of spreading and regeneration following cutting or grazing exhibited by grasses afford the prospect of developing perennial crops requiring a minimum of labour and producing regular and rich yields with a high content of carbohydrates and proteins, vitamins and other biologically valuable active substances. Perennial strains of wheat and other cereals have already been developed but cultivating them in practice still poses problems. Experts have been successful in obtaining high-yielding varieties of wheat and other cereals, in obtaining the hybrid, 'Triticale' by interbreeding wheat and rye, and in obtaining the corn strain 'Opaque' with a composition of amino-acids comparable only to that afforded by animal proteins or soya.

On the principle of the seasonal rhythmic cycle, that is the ability to react to the various seasons of the year, it is possible to observe in grasses many laws, which if mastered could lead to far greater yields obtained than has been possible to date. Meadow Fox-tail commences growth early in spring and some years flowers as soon as April. Regeneration following cutting, however, is poor. On the other hand, Cocksfoot, likewise an early-growing grass, regenerates within a short time by putting out a great number of vegetative (leaf) shoots. Most bents have their main growth period in summer so that they are used as aftermath grazing and hay crops. Attempts to make Fox-tail regenerate abundantly or to obtain early growth in bents have so far met with no success. Similarly in the case of grasses with vigorous growth and rapidly hardening tissues it has not been found possible to delay the onset of lignification, for example, until after the flowering period.

The differing ability of the various species and varieties of grasses to react to various external conditions is inherited and can be changed only by changing the plant's genetically conditioned constitution and characteristics. As things stand at present we must be governed by the requirements of the grasses and adapt our objectives to the possibilities afforded by the individual species and also by the varied composition of grassland. The species composition of grassland is also influenced by natural competition and selection in the plant community, which is why certain species may be crowded out or may become dominant. In forest communities, added to these mutual influences, which are called allelopathic, is the influence of the root secretions and mycorrhizas of woody plants. Also, an important factor influencing the growth of grass in woodland is the amount of light that reaches the forest floor.

As has already been stated, the emergence of a young plant and its entire ensuing development is a chain of extremely complex life functions, one following upon the other. It starts with germination — which marks the first sign of life inside the seed. Given a favourable temperature and an adequate supply of moisture for a sufficient length of time, water eventually penetrates to the embryo resulting in the activation of physiological processes. This initiates the release of the enzyme amylase (diastase) through the cotyledon or scutellum, located between the embryo and the starchy endosperm, which gradually converts the starch in the endosperm into sugar. The sugar then passes through the scutellum to the embryo and together with other dissolved substances provides the food and energy for the growth and initial development of the embryo. These processes take place inside the seed. Most important at this stage of germination is the influence of water and temperature, which together with other external factors affect the formation of the organs inside the seed.

Actual germination starts with the emergence of the radicle or root, which begins to absorb water from the soil and grows positively geotropically, that is, downwards in response to gravity. Soon after that, root hairs develop at the root tip to provide the growing embryo with a further supply of food. The young seedling is still below the surface of the ground and thus obtains its food heterotrophically, absorbing not only mineral substances from the soil but also energy-rich organic materials from its reserves. For this reason an adequate supply of oxygen in the soil as well as an adequate supply of water is very important at this stage. In the first days of growth and development the root begins to branch and forms a number of secondary or adventitious roots, which develop in various ways according to the depth at which the seed is sown. The emergence of the root is followed by the emergence of the plumule which gives rise to a vegetative shoot that pushes its way upwards through the soil. As soon as the plant has its first green leaf germination is at an end; the plant ceases to be heterotrophic and becomes autotrophic, which means that food for further growth is fabricated by the plant itself by photosynthesis.

Increase in size is the next stage in the development of young grass plants. They either form tufts or else spread by means of surface stems (stolons) or underground stems (rhizomes), which may be short or long.

Coming into ear is the stage of growth when the inflorescences, for example, spikes or panicles, begin to form in the topmost leaf sheaths. This stage is followed by a further lengthy period of growth until the whole inflorescence emerges from the leaf sheath and begins to flower.

When grasses flower the spikelets and florets open, the filaments of the stamens elongate rapidly, pushing the anthers out over the sides of the floret, and at the same time the two feathery stigmas grow and project from the floret. The filaments of the stamens elongate so rapidly that their growth may be seen with the naked eye, for instance in the spikes of rye. Grasses are almost always pollinated by the wind, in which case they are said to be anemophilous. Ripe pollen grains are often carried great distances by the wind before being deposited on and adhering to a sticky stigma.

Deposition of the pollen grain is soon followed by the first signs of its germination and the formation of a pollen tube. This is initiated by specific substances secreted by the stigma. As a result of chemotaxis, or response to the chemical composition of the substances in the stigma and style, the pollen tube grows down through the loose tissue of the style until it reaches and ruptures the embryo sac inside which the male and female gametes fuse to form the zygote, or fertilized egg cell. Ensuing cell division transforms the fertilized egg cell into an embryo. This is followed by the formation of the layers that form the seed coat and the pericarp to yield the final product — the fruit or grain. This method of reproduction is known as sexual reproduction.

Grasses often multiply also by asexual or vegetative means. Even those species which are distinguished by sexual reproduction generally multiply in summer by vegetative means as well. Grasses that spread only during the main growing season, that is, usually during the month of May, form the basis for once-harvested meadows. Grasses that put out stems repeatedly even in the summer months form the basis for twice-harvested and multi-harvested meadows.

Seeds sometimes germinate very early, in damp weather even while still in the spoke or panicle. Some grasses may be viviparous, that is, miniature plants are formed directly in the spikelets on the parent plant, for example certain species of meadow-grass.

GRASS-GROWING REGIONS

From the biological and agricultural points of view grasses are the most important group of plants in the world. Their outstanding powers of competition in plant communities have enabled them to retain their predominance in widely varied situations. In regions with a very short growth period because of insufficient warmth or moisture, grasses are of inestimable importance. The rapid growth and development of certain species in harsh climates ensure the establishment of certain species or practically continuous grasslands which in mountain, steppe, semi-desert and occasionally even in desert areas can be used for temporary grazing, thus providing the basis for agricultural production even in inhospitable regions.

Grasses may be found in the Alps at heights of more than 3 000 metres (almost 10 000 ft). They grow beyond the Arctic Circle, in places with salty soil, on volcanic and alluvial deposits, as well as on cliffs, roadsides, railway embankments and motorway verges. Grasses prevent erosion on steep hillsides, consolidate coastal sand dunes, dry out peat bogs and fens, strengthen river and pond banks and together with mosses and lichens are pioneer plants on cliffs and screes.

Probably nowhere in the world is there a large plant association in which grasses do not play an important part and in the tropics, subtropics and cold regions they are widely distributed.

Savannas, which are vast grasslands stretching in Africa from the Sahara to the desert plateau Kalahari, contain huge stands of widely varied grasses, mainly various species of *Pennisetum, Andropogon,*

Panicum and *Aristida*. The South American savannas, stretching from the Cordilleras to the Orinoco and Ecuador, are also dense grasslands made up chiefly of *Andropogon*, *Aristida* and many species of sedges. Conditions in the tropical regions of Asia are no different. The savannas of India are noted for the vast stands of the hard *Imperata* grass. The Asian steppes contain vast stands of fescues and bromes which together with *Stipa* grasses give this region with its dry inland climate its specific character. In tropical Australia the savannas contain in addition to *Andropogon* and *Panicum* many grasses of the genus *Eragrostis*, *Sporobolus*, and others. Even in milder steppe and prairie climates grasses are the most important of all plants.

The South American pampas are particularly rich in grasses. When in flower the vast stands of tall Pampas Grass and *Stipa* grasses form an endless expanse of glittering silver panicles. The North American prairies are also characterized by drought-resistant grasses, mostly of the genus *Stipa*, *Aristida*, *Spartina* and *Panicum*. Buffalo Grass (*Buchloe dactyloides*) also forms large continuous carpets.

Grasslands are also to be found in Europe and neighbouring islands. In the mild climate of Europe the cultivated meadow and pasture grasslands are most important. Here will be found the grasses of field and forest and in drier regions also large steppe grasslands, for instance, in southern and south-eastern Europe. Europe's meadows are an important factor in contributing to the greenness of the entire continent, including the coastal areas in the north and south, the inland reaches with their mild climate, and the rocky heights of the mountains.

CHOOSING THE GRASS FOR A LAWN

Grasses, particularly cereals, have been held in high esteem since ancient times and used as fodder in natural pastures and meadow lands. Contributing to the beauty and general appearance of the landscape grasses are a permanent part of man's environment, both that which is shaped by him as well as in virgin nature. They play an important part in the landscaping of grounds and gardens, forming compact turf, lawns or garden features when grown as solitary specimens. Their beauty resides in their shape, slenderness, remarkable structure, delicate inflorescence, long, graceful stems or short, dwarf habit.

Grasses have served man as a source of artistic inspiration. The art of the Far East, the ikebana-style flower arrangement, paintings on porcelain and silk, are all in substance a hymn to the beauty and daintiness of the perfect shapes and movements that can be conjured up only by the leaves, stems and panicles of grasses.

Grasses are increasingly being put to practical use throughout the world. Fine lawns, sports-ground turf, grasses on roadsides and alongside lanes are remarkably long-lived communities tolerating long-term wear by treading as well as temporary damage, and in favourable climates retaining their fresh green colour throughout the year.

Establishing a lawn is not very difficult. It can even be purchased ready-made and simply rolled out on previously prepared soil. Grass mixtures may be sown by hand but they may also be distributed under pressure with a jet of water on to steep banks bordering highways, ponds, lakes and dams.

Like all plant cultures a lawn has specific requirements for good growth and development and the selection of the species and varieties of grasses for mixtures is determined by the local climatic conditions and the purpose they are to serve. The grasses that are most commonly used in seed mixtures for fine lawns are: Smooth Meadow-grass, Perennial Rye-grass, Red Fescue, Common Bent, Crested Dog's-tail, Smaller Cat's-tail, Black Bent, Creeping Bent, Rough Meadow-grass, Wood Meadow-grass, Flattened Meadow-grass, Wood Hair-grass, Sheep's Fescue and Annual Meadow-grass.

For fine lawn the proportion should be 35–70 grams of seed mixture per square metre (1–2 ozs per sq. yd). Low-growing Smooth Meadow-grass and Red Fescue generally form the bulk of mixtures for such a lawn. Added to this is a smaller portion of Common Bent and Creeping Bent for good growth in summer and a small amount of Perennial Rye-grass may be added for rapid coverage of the area. In very poor and dry sandy soils the inclusion of a greater portion of Sheep's Fescue in place of Smooth Meadow-grass is recommended. For average conditions the following mixture should be sown to obtain a fine turf: 50 per cent Red Fescue, 25 per cent Smooth Meadow-grass, 12·5 per cent Common Bent and 12·5 per cent Perennial Rye-grass.

For shaded areas the mixture should contain species that tolerate shade and partial shade, particularly Wood Meadow-grass, Wood Hair-grass, Creeping Bent, Sheep's Fescue and Rough Meadow-grass. The following mixture is recommended : 40 per cent Wood Meadow-grass, 20 per cent Red and Chewings Fescue, 30 per cent Wood Hair-grass and 10 per cent Common Bent. Sheep's Fescue and Rough Meadow-grass may also be included in the mixture.

Mixtures used for heavily trodden sports fields and paths have to be able to regenerate rapidly and require well-aerated, oxygen-rich soil for development of the roots. The bulk of such mixtures is again formed by Smooth Meadow-grass (low, rapidly regenerating strains), Red Fescue and Common Bent. Added to this are Annual Meadow-grass, Crested Dog's-tail and, in damper situations, Creeping Bent. Annual Meadow-grass, which quickly forms a grass cover, is good for repairing damage to lawn surfaces. The proportion of grasses is 37·5 per cent Smooth Meadow-grass, 25 per cent Red Fescue, 25 per cent Common Bent and 12·5 per cent of any of the other kinds. The bulk of mixtures advocated for the verges of motorways, roadsides, ponds and the like is again formed by Smooth Meadow-grass and Red Fescue. Growth of the grass cover in the summer months is assured by the presence of Common Bent and in damp soils by Creeping Bent aud Velvet Bent. Rough Meadow-grass, Black Bent, Wood Hair-grass and Flattened Meadow-grass are good supplements.

Grasses planted as ornamentals include more than 100 species and varieties, ranging from miniature fescues only a few centimetres high to several-metres-high Pampas Grass, which is grown either as a solitary specimen or in groups.

Very low growth is a characteristic found chiefly amongst fescues *(Festuca glacialis, F. tenuifolia, F. valesiaca, F. glauca)*, bents *(Agrostis rupestris, A. alpina)* and other grasses, many of which belong to other families such as rushes and sedges. Tall and slender grasses such as *Molinia altissima, Calamagrostis epigeois hortorum, C. arundinacea purpurea, Stipa gigantea* and others are put out in ornamental gardens either as solitary specimens or in groups.

Robust solitary specimens include chiefly *Cortaderia*

selloana, Spartina michauxiana aureomarginata, Miscanthus sacchariflorus robustus and other *Miscanthus* species, as well as species of the genera *Phragmites* and *Bambusa*.

Ornamental grasses that remain green throughout the year include *Festuca amethystina, F. gigantea, F. glauca, F. tenuifolia, Sesleria heuffeliana, Arundinaria japonica, Bambusa nitida, B. simonii* and *B. metake*. Grasses noted for their lovely coloration include species of *Miscanthus, Molinia altissima, Phalaris arundinacea picta, Festuca glauca, Arrhenatherum bulbosum variegatum, Calamagrostis arundinacea purpurea, Glyceria spectabilis variegata, Spartina michauxiana aureomarginata* and colour varieties of maize.

Noteworthy for the shape of the tufts they make, their inflorescence or fruits are the ornamental grasses *Briza maxima, Coix lacryma-jobi, Panicum capillare, P. clandestinum* and varieties of maize with coloured grains. The annual grasses *Lagurus ovatus* and *Pennisetum alupecuroides* are extremely lovely and delicate.

ESTABLISHING AND CARING FOR A LAWN

Fine lawns, sports fields, grassy paths and other areas with compact grass cover require special care. Successful results depend to a great extent on the climatic conditions. A moist atmosphere and adequate light are the basic requirements. To remain in good condition for many years the grass must also be provided with good, well-aerated soil containing the required nutrients in balanced proportion.

The first step in creating a good lawn is to prepare the soil with rake and hoe to obtain a fine and crumbly tilth and enrich it with humus and mineral foods. Proprietary feeds should be added to the soil at least a month before sowing.

The best time to sow seed is in autumn from mid-August to mid-September, provided the weather is neither too dry nor too wet for the ground to be properly prepared. Seed can also be sown in spring, in which case April is the best month to choose. The soil should be well moistened before sowing, since unless the weather is very dry it is not advisable to water again until after germination has taken place.

Seed should be sown at the rate of approximately 35 to 70 grams per square metre (1–2 ozs per sq.yd). To ensure even distribution, it may be helpful to divide the ground into metre-wide strips or squares and measure out the correct proportions of seed. Sand or sawdust added to the seed may also aid even distribution. The seed can be spread either by hand or from a wheeled distributor which can be pre-set to discharge the correct amount.

After sowing, the seed should be covered by a layer of finely sifted soil or by raking and cross-raking the ground, or it can be lightly rolled in with a light-weight roller. This should be sufficient protection against the deprivations of birds since most grass seed nowadays is pre-treated with a bird deterrent.

Most grasses will have germinated within a week to ten days and all that is then necessary is to water the new grass lightly as required. When it is about 10 centimetres (4 ins) high watering should be limited and the grass cut with a sharp scythe or sickle, or with razor-sharp mower blades. The first topping should be done with great care with the mower blades set high for the roots are not yet well anchored.

Aftercare is the same as for established lawns. To keep turf thick and green it must not only be watered regularly but also provided with regular applications of fertilizer. This should be done at least three times a year, the total amount equalling about 3 kilograms of feed per 100 square metres (5·5 lbs per 100 sq.yds). The special feeds used for this purpose usually consist of a mixture of the basic nutrients, that is nitrogen, phosphoric acid and potassium oxide with traces of ferric chloride. The first application in spring should be given in liquid form, dissolved in water according to the manufacturer's instructions, and then two or three times in the course of the season, always following rainfall or thorough watering and after mowing.

It is very important to keep the turf supplied with oxygen and old and well-trodden lawns should be aerated with an aerator, a spiked tool for making holes in the ground which enables oxygen to penetrate to the grass roots and underground stems. Aerating the lawn is particularly important in spring when removing moss. Small areas can be spiked with an ordinary garden fork. Afterwards the turf should be rolled with a light-weight roller so the lifted roots are pressed back into the soil.

The time for weed control is early in spring. This may be done by hand removal or chemical treatment with any of the many herbicides available for this purpose. Bald or damaged parts of established lawns should be scratched up and sown with a seed mixture as in preparing a new lawn.

An established lawn should be mown regularly so that the grass is no higher than 7 centimetres (3 ins), otherwise the turf becomes thin and weak. Regular mowing, watering and feeding are the three musts for a lush, handsome lawn which can be given ornamental touches either by mowing always in one direction, or up and down to form contrasting bands or even in a chequerboard pattern.

CLASSIFICATION OF GRASSES

For easy reference the grasses described in this book are grouped according to genera and the genera arranged not according to the botanical system but according to the type of inflorescence as follows: raceme or true spike (plates no. 1 to 14), very narrow spike-like panicle (plates no. 15 to 26, 40), panicle with one-flowered, occasionally two-flowered spikelets (plates no. 27 to 39, 41 to 44), panicle with multi-flowered, awnless spikelets (plates no. 45 to 61,63 and 64), panicle with multi-flowered, awned spikelets (plates no. 62, 65 to 77), panicle with spikelets furnished with bent awns (plates no. 78 to 82), grasses of distinctive external appearance with inflorescences generally different from the described types (plates no. 83 to 88).

After classifying a given grass according to the type of inflorescence, detailed external characteristics of the inflorescence, spikelets, the leaves and culms should be examined, and sometimes also whether it is rhizomatous or stoloniferous, for otherwise it is impossible to identify the various grasses with any degree of certainty.

PLATES

Slender or Wood False-brome

Brachypodium silvaticum (HUDS.) BEAUV.   Poaceae

Wood False-brome is a shallow-rooted perennial grass which forms large tufts in spring and flowers in summer. The culms are tall and erect, slender, pendent at the tip and hairy at the nodes. The ligules are up to 4 millimetres (0·16 in.) long and toothed at the end. The spikelets are more than 2 centimetres (0·8 in.) long, and unlike Rye-grass, oval in cross-section. The leaves are a fresh green, and the blade is broad.

The chief distinguishing feature is the inflorescence, which is a spike-like raceme with short branches only about 2 to 3 millimetres (0·1 in.) long. It is pendent and furnished with long awns.

This grass is suitable for shady woods and humus-rich soils. It is found in Europe and Asia from lowlands to mountains. It has no special light or temperature requirements and is common in shady, especially damp woods and thickets, and in parks and gardens. It is a handsome grass and with its compact tufts would also be useful as an ornamental grass. It remains fresh and green throughout the summer until autumn.

Its importance as fodder is negligible; it is not very nutritious. In some localities it may be found to contain a large concentration of cyanogenic glycosides, that is, substances which through the action of enzymes release hydrocyanic acid, which is poisonous, so that if animals feed only on this grass it may prove dangerous. It is not usually grazed by cattle because they find its toughness and hairiness unpleasant.

a) vegetative part of the plant
b) culm with pendent inflorescence
c) detail of ligule and node

a

c

b

Chalk or Heath False-brome

Brachypodium pinnatum (L.) BEAUV.   Poaceae

Chalk False-brome is a moss-green perennial grass with characteristic creeping rhizomes. It is of medium height and resembles Wood False-brome. The nodes have soft hairs, the lower leaf sheaths are short-haired. The inflorescence is a raceme; the spikelets have short awns.

Important distinguishing characteristics are the upright habit, the multi-flowered spikelets all inclined at the same angle away from the stem, the short-awned lemmas and the short leaf-ligules. The rhizomes, spreading several centimetres below the surface of the soil, form loose stands or circumscribed masses of this grass.

Chalk False-brome is found throughout Europe, in temperate Asia and in North Africa. It thrives primarily at lower levels, though it also occurs in mountains, but requires more light and warmth than Wood False-brome. It holds the soil on banks and is often found growing on the edges of woods. It is regarded as an indicator of calcareous soils even though it may also grow in places without lime.

Agriculturally the Wood False-brome is of little worth. Young and tender plants are grazed by cattle but during the flowering period, in summer, the grass is tough and of less value, and may even be harmful. Toxic cyanogenic glycosides are just as likely to be present in this grass as in Wood False-brome.

a) vegetative part of the plant
b) inflorescence
c) detail of section of leaf with ligule

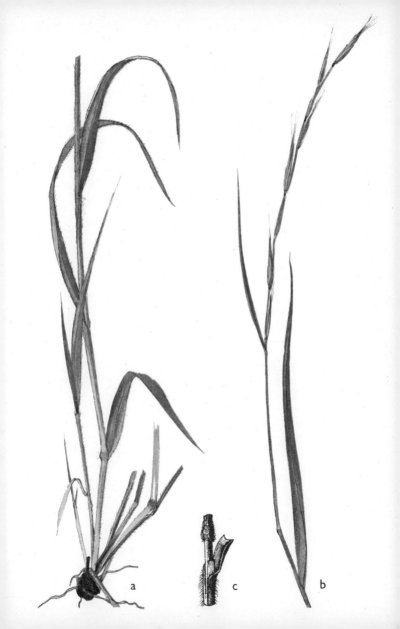

a   c   b

Couch-grass or Twitch

Agropyron repens (L.) BEAUV.   Poaceae

Couch-grass is a perennial weed of meadow, field and garden. The chief distinguishing features are the large, white or yellowish, sharply pointed rhizomes, the short-awned or sharply pointed lemmas of the multi-flowered spikelets, and the well-developed coiled half-auricles on the leaves. The ligules are extremely short but two auricles are well developed. The leaf-blades may become rolled.

Couch-grass is widespread throughout Europe and Asia, particularly on cultivated, humus-rich soils. Abundance of this grass causes drying up of the soil and a marked decrease in the yield of cultivated crops.

The rhizomes spread through the soil even penetrating soft obstacles such as potato tubers or other plant parts. It is these rhizomes that make Couch-grass such a troublesome weed and very difficult to eradicate. Only by applying chemical herbicides has it been posssible to prevent its mass occurrence on cultivated land. When allowed to grow freely on arable land Couch-grass forms a loose cover of green or greyish green leafy shoots. The spikes flower in June to July. The spikelets are placed with their broader side to the axis and are distinguished by more or less pointed glumes.

Couch-grass can be used as feed for pigs and is nutritionally very valuable in meadow grasslands. The rhizomes have a medicinal effect.

a) basal part of the plant with rhizomes
b) inflorescence
c) spike with spikelets with broader side appressed to the axis
d) detail of auricle at the junction of leaf-blade and leaf-sheath

36

a   d   c   b

Sand Couch-grass

Agropyron junceiforme (LÖVE) LÖVE   Poaceae

Sand Couch-grass is a perennial coastal grass spreading
extensively by rhizomes. The leaves are bluish green,
the culms about 60 centimetres (23 ins) high. The spikes,
which may be as much as 20 centimetres (8 ins) long,
depending on the fertility of the soil, are stout, awnless,
and greyish green. The leaf-blades are covered with
fine hairs on the upper surface.

Distinguishing factors are the bluish colouring, awnless
spikelets arranged in a loose spike and glumes with
a whitish waxy margin. The glumes are about two-thirds
the length of the spikelets and have prominent nerves,
seven to nine vascular bundles. The stout rhizomes spread
great distances and form intermittent loose or dense masses together with other species of coastal grasses.

Sand Couch-grass is widespread in Europe. Its range
of distribution extends from the north to the Adriatic
Sea but does not include Iceland. It grows also on the
coastal dunes of North Africa and Asia Minor.

Agriculturally, Sand Couch-grass is of little worth. During the flowering period (June to August) the plants
become very tough and the leaves roll in dry weather.
It is, however, very good for holding together coastal
sands and assisting the formation of sand dunes for it
appreciates high concentrations of salt in the soil. In
soils with a low concentration of salt it soon dies.

a) basal part of the plant
b) culm with spike
c) detail of junction of leaf-blade and leaf-sheath

c

a   b

Bearded Couch-grass

Agropyron caninum (L.) BEAUV.   Poaceae

Bearded Couch-grass is a perennial plant. The culms, bearing characteristic awned spikelets, are up to 150 centimetres (59 ins) high. The spikes are usually pendent, particularly after flowering has finished. The leaves are grey-green above and dark glossy green below. The ligules are short and truncated.

Identification characteristics are the awned lemmas, the awns being longer than the lemmas. The spike breaks readily and as in other couch grasses the spikelets are pressed closely with their broader side to the axis. The plants form loose tufts without rhizomes, and the peak flowering season is in June and July.

Bearded Couch-grass grows throughout Europe, except in Portugal and Turkey, as well as in western Asia and North America. It is a grass found mainly in lightly shaded places on damp, humus-rich soils, doing best in damp woods, coastal thickets and near water courses both in lowlands and at higher levels.

This grass is of little agricultural worth for it soon becomes tough and grows in inaccessible places. It can be used only for occasional grazing. Though it may irritate the alimentary passages when grazed during the flowering and fruiting periods because the spike breaks up easily, it is otherwise harmless.

a) vegetative part of the plant
b) culm with spike
c) detail of section of leaf with ligule

40

c

a   b

Perennial Rye-grass

Lolium perenne L. Poaceae

Perennial Rye-grass is a glossy dark-green perennial forming dense tufts with 40–70 centimetre (16–28 ins)
culms and flowering from May to September. The spikes
are long and slender, the spikelets multi-flowered and
arranged with their narrow edges against the axis.

The main distinguishing feature is the awnless spikelets
with glumes up to two-thirds of their length.

Perennial Rye-grass is a popular grass cultivated the
world over and it has been grown in England since the
seventeenth century. It is valuable for grazing and hay-
making, and also for ornamental lawns and sports fields.
It grows rapidly after cutting, stands up well to trampling
and treading and together with White and Red Clovers
forms the basis for rich pastures. During the flowering
period the culms rapidly harden and in communities
where there are taller plants this grass often suffers from
lack of light. Its many good qualities and wide range of
uses as well as its comparative ease of cultivation make
Perennial Rye-grass, together with Smooth Meadow-
grass, one of the most valuable cultivated grasses.

a) basal part of the plant
b) culm with spike
c) detail of flowering spikelet
d) detail of flower stalk

b   d   a

c

Italian Rye-grass

Lolium multiflorum LAM.   Poaceae

Italian Rye-grass is an annual or biennial grass of rapid growth forming pale green tufts and flowering in early summer. The inflorescence is a spike consisting of awned, multi-flowered spikelets arranged with their narrow edges against the axis. The chief distinguishing characteristics are the awned spikelets and short glumes only half the length of the spikelets.

A native of western Europe, this grass is frequently cultivated. It is grown for fodder, for ornamental lawns and in meadows and often occurs in the wild. It makes rapid growth even at low temperatures, so that it is a good grass for the harsher climate of mountain foothills. However, it does not stand up well to lack of oxygen and often dies if covered by snow for a lengthy period. It is extremely valuable as a fodder plant, mostly because it is so highly productive, and is noted for its high yield at first harvesting. It is also much valued for its high seed output, which is the highest of all grasses.

Of the many varieties the best known is *L. annuum* var. *westerwoldicum*, noted for its rapid development, growth and good response to feeding. The other cultivated varieties are grown mostly as fodder plants and not for ornamental purposes.

a) basal part of the plant
b) flowering spike
c) detail of spikelet

a   b   c

Darnel

Lolium temulentum L.   Poaceae

Darnel is an annual grass often coloured bluish green which grows to a height of 40–70 centimetres (16–28 ins). The culms are stout and rough at the top, and the spikes robust, with awned, multi-flowered spikelets. The leaves are rough on the upper surface and smooth below. The upper leaf-sheaths are slightly inflated.

The main distinguishing marks are the long awns and the glumes, which are the same length or longer than the spikelets. The awns may be straight or bent.

Though not itself toxic, Darnel may be regarded as a poisonous plant because it is often infested by the poisonous parasitic fungus *Stomatinia temulenta*. The mycelium of this fungus is found mainly in the seeds, which are the most poisonous part of the infested plant. The toxicity is caused by the alkaloid temuline, which passes into the water when the plant is soaked, thus making the fluid extract poisonous as well. The poison affects the optic nerve and causes vertigo and spasms. Darnel is found throughout Europe excepting the northernmost parts, and occurs only rarely in Britain. It is widespread in Asia, Africa and other continents. In former times it was also a common weed of spring cereal crops and a dreaded poisonous plant. Nowadays, thanks mainly to the cleanliness of seeds used in sowing, it is fast disappearing in countries with a developed agriculture. It is noted, however, for the extremely long germinating viability of its seeds.

a) vegetative part of plant
b) culm with spike
c) detail of long-awned spikelet

a   c   b

Meadow Barley

Hordeum secalinum SCHREB.   Poaceae

Meadow Barley is a tufted perennial grass coloured
greyish green. The flower-bearing culms which are formed from June to August, are 30–70 centimetres (12–28
ins) high and may be erect or bent at the base. The
lower leaf-sheaths are covered with short stiff hairs, the
blades are narrow, sometimes inrolled, and bristle-like.
The base of the stem may be swollen. The spike is 3–5
centimetres (1–2 ins) long, cylindrical, with an axis that
breaks up at maturity. The lateral glumes are trans-
formed into awns, often more than 10 millimetres (0·4 in.)
long.

Typical characteristics are the bulbous base of the stem,
the lower leaf-sheaths, the long upper, leafless part of
the stem, and the cylindrical spike with stalked glumes
that serve as awns.

Meadow Barley grows chiefly in damp meadows,
coastal and river marshlands and also on higher ground,
up to 1 000 metres (3 280 ft) above sea level. It is
distributed in the warmer regions of Europe and Asia,
from where it has also made its way to the African and
American continents. Its range is continually expanding
for it even tolerates soil with a high concentration of
salt. It forms loose, continuous growths. It dries quickly
and then mars the appearance of the landscape, so that
it is regarded as an unwelcome weed.

It is not of much worth as forage but can be used for
spring grazing. Later it rapidly becomes tough and because of its awns may cause illness and even death in cattle.

a) vegetative part of the plant showing bulbous base
b) culm with spike
c) detail of spikelet

a   c   b

Wall Barley

Hordeum murinum L.   Poaceae

Wall Barley is an annual, though often overwintering, grass, with long-awned spikes reminiscent of cultivated barley. It grows to a height of 40 centimetres (16 ins), sometimes even 1 metre (39 ins) on fertile soils.

The chief distinguishing features are the axis which breaks up at maturity and the central lemma which is awl-shaped, long-awned and fringed with hairs. The lemmas of the lateral spikelets differ in being much narrower.

This is an early spring grass of fairly rapid growth. It is very tolerant of drought and grows in tufts on both fertile and poor soils. It often forms large masses on village commons and waysides and beside walls, occurring in lowlands, mountain valleys and by the coast. It is widespread throughout practically the whole world, though absent in Iceland and Albania.

When young, before producing ears, it is good as food for stock. From the time the ears are formed, however, it is unsafe for animals because the scratchy awns form indigestible clumps in the digestive tract which may even cause the animal's death. When it ripens, Wall Barley turns yellow to brownish and spoils the appearance of the ground where it occurs. Unlike this weed, some barleys, for instance Fox-tail Barley (*H. jubatum*), with its lovely fan-shaped spikes, are highly ornamental.

a) basal part of the plant
b) culm with spike
c) detail of flowering spikelet with characteristic central awned glume

a   b   c

Sea Barley or Squirrel-tail Grass

Hordeum marinum HUDS.   Poaceae

Sea Barley is a tufted annual with leaves and culms coloured greyish-green. In early summer it forms numerous culms, 20–40 centimetres (8–16 ins) high, terminated by cylindrical spikes with awns of medium length. Unlike other wild barleys Sea Barley has leaves up to the axis of the spike. The glumes of the central spikelets are rough-haired.

Sea Barley grows on salty meadows and along the sea coast. It is a very common species in the warmer parts and western coasts of Europe, as far as Dalmatia and including Britain, but absent in eastern and northern Europe. Two subspecies occur: *H. marinum eumaritimum* is a native of south-western Europe and is distinguished by the glumes of its lateral spikes being of the same length but having dissimilar awns. *H. marinum hystrix*, found as far as central Europe and growing mostly on salt flats, is also distinguished by the fact that the glumes on the lateral spikelets are the same length but the awn of the lemma of the central spikelet is longer than the glumes of the lateral spikelets. Sea Barley was formerly classified as *Zeocrithon maritimum*.

After flowering is finished the entire plant dries. As food for stock it is of little worth or even harmful like the other barleys which grow as weeds, nor is it particularly attractive to look at.

a) basal part of the plant
b) culm with spike
c) detail of spikelet with rough central glumes

a

b

c

Lyme Grass

Elymus arenarius L.   Poaceae

Lyme Grass is a robust, bluish, coastal perennial more
than 1 metre (39 ins) high (on fertile soil it may grow as
high as 2 metres (78 ins). It spreads by long, stout rhizomes which give rise to dense growths. The flowering
period is from June to August. The stout culms are terminated by dense awnless spikelets arranged in a terminal
spike. The leaves are broad with pointed auricles but
without ligules. The culms are smooth, or rough just
below the spike, and thickly clad with reflexed hairs at
the nodes. The leaf-sheaths are likewise smooth, the
upper sheaths slightly inflated.

Lyme Grass is distinguished by the bluish colour of the
above-ground parts, the absence of awns on the spikelets,
their hairiness, the longitudinal grooves on the leaf-
blades and the stout rhizomes.

It forms extensive covers and is effective in binding sand
dunes in the cooler coastal areas of Europe. It is absent
only on the Mediterranean coast. The seed, or grain,
may also be used as food. When cooked it is just as
nourishing and tastes much the same as rice.

Lyme Grass resembles Wood Barley (*E. europaeus*) but
the latter is coloured grass-green, grows in woods and
does not have rhizomes. Both are useful ornamental
grasses for the garden, particularly when grown as solitary
specimens in the same way as the central European
species, *E. caput-medusae*.

a) basal part of the plant
b) spike
c) detail of junction of leaf-blade and leaf-sheath with auricles
   and atrophied ligule

Matgrass

Nardus stricta L.

Poaceae

Matgrass is a densely tufted perennial with stiff, erect stems growing in connected rows from short, stout rhizomes. It bears interesting, one-sided, comb-like spikes in late spring. The small spikelets are one-flowered with three anthers but only one stigma instead of the usual two of most grasses. The basal leaf-sheaths are a glossy yellow-brown, the others greenish grey. The blades are thin, rough, and bristle-like.

Distinguishing marks are the tufts of closely packed rows of stems, the thin, bristle-like, rolled leaves and the one-sided, comb-like inflorescence made up of one-flowered, awned spikelets.

Matgrass is widespread throughout Europe. It is intolerant of lime and is found in places poor in nitrogen, on acidic mountain and lowland soils, chiefly heaths, moors and similar places.

Matgrass often forms a pure grass cover which tolerates very acidic, poor soils and a harsh climate such as in mountain regions. In such places it may be grazed by cattle and sheep if no other food is available. It is an important component of shallow heath and mountain vegetation for it prevents erosion by wind and water.

a) tuft with vegetative shoots and flower-bearing culms
b) detail of flower with single stigma
c) detail of spikelet

a

b

c

Sea Hard-grass

Parapholis strigosa (DUM.) C. E. HUBBARD.   Poaceae

Sea Hard-grass is a small, annual grass forming loose tufts of prostrate or slightly curved and ascending whip-like shoots. The flower heads — slender, stiff spikes consisting of one-flowered spikelets — are borne from April till July, very occasionally even later. The spikelets are embedded in hollows in the spike axis so that the inflorescence is practically unnoticeable. The spikelets are awnless, about 6–7 millimetres (about 0·25 in.) long, and arranged alternately with their broader edges against the spike axis. The leaves are awl-shaped; only at the beginning of development are they flat. The sheaths are tightly clasped around the stem and the ligules are membranous. The spike is about 10 centimetres (4 ins) long and is very similar in appearance to the vegetative shoots.

The chief features are the slender, stiff spikes with joined axis, the one-flowered spikelets and the occurrence of the grass on salty, poor, sandy or stony soils.

This grass is widely distributed along the coasts of southern Europe, excepting Albania, and grows well also on the salty sands and coastal cliffs of western Europe. It is common in Asia as well. This is a salt-loving weed of no value whatsoever, being of no use either as forage or as a binder of shifting coastal sands. In botanical literature it is also classified as *Pholiurus filiformis* and *Lepturus filiformis*.

a) the plant's habit
b) detail of section of spike

a

b

Crested Dog's-tail

Cynosurus cristatus L.   Poaceae

Crested Dog's tail is a fresh green perennial grass about
50 centimetres (20 ins) high. It forms compact tufts of
slender, erect culms terminated by contracted, one-sided,
spike-like panicles with a characteristic comb-like arrangement. This is composed of two kinds of spikelets, fertile
and sterile. The leaf-sheaths are entire, the blades grooved
and usually rolled, the ligules short and collar-like. The
chief distinction is the crest-like, narrow, spike-like
panicle.

Crested Dog's tail is widespread throughout practically
all Europe and part of Asia and as a cultivated grass in
all continents. In the wild it grows in pastures and meadows as well as in open places in woods, particularly at
higher levels. In harsher mountain climates and in the
north it is valued as a hardy grass with good spreading properties which tolerates damp, peaty soils as well as dry situations. The culms soon harden and are bypassed by grazing cattle, leaving the spikelets to ripen and enabling the
grass to seed itself and spread. Because of its attractive
habit and ease of growth, Crested Dog's-tail is often used
with other grasses in the formation of lawns where it
firms the turf and improves resistance to treading. It
stands up well to the dry weather of the summer months.

a) the plant's habit
b) culm with panicle
c) detail of leaf with short, collar-like ligule

b   c   a

Timothy Grass

Phleum pratense L.   Poaceae

This is a densely tufted perennial grass with short, creeping rhizomes which flowers from June till August. The culms grow to a height of more than 1 metre (39 ins) and are terminated by a dense, spike-like panicle about 10 centimetres (4 ins) long. Unlike the Purple-stem Cat's-tail (*P. phleoides*) it does not form lobes along the outer edge when bent over the finger. The spikelets are compressed, the glumes are short-awned, the lemma and palea awnless. The leaf-blades are flat, the sheaths smooth and the ligules of the upper leaves up to 5 millimetres (0·2 in.) long and irregularly toothed.

The chief distinguishing factors are the glumes having keels fringed with stiff hairs, the culms having swollen bases, and the narrow, cylindrical, spike-like panicle. During the flowering period the anthers are purplish.

This is a common cultivated European grass found on fertile soil on both low and high ground. It responds well to the application of fertilizers, tolerates acid soils and requires a fair amount of light and moisture. It is grown extensively in meadows and pastures where it remains soft and fresh for a long time. In view of its good growth properties numerous strains of this grass have been bred for meadow, pasture and field cultivation. In the wild, particularly in open grassy areas, it is very decorative and is regarded as a grass that improves the look of the landscape.

a) basal part of the plant
b) culm with spike-like panicle
c) detail of spikelet with awned glumes
d) culm of the Purple-stem Cat's-tail with bent and lobed spike-like panicle

d   a   b

Sand Cat's-tail

Phleum arenarium L.   Poaceae

The Sand Cat's-tail is a small, annual grass growing to a height of about 10 centimetres (4 ins). On very poor soils the flower-bearing culms are only 5 centimetres (2 ins) high, on more fertile soils up to 25 centimetres (10 ins) high. The flowering period is from May till July. All the culms are terminated by an ovoid or slightly cylindrical spike-like panicle only 2–3 centimetres (about 1 in.) long. The spikelets are very small with short hairs on the keels; the lemmas have short awn-like tips. The leaf-blades are short and broad at the base, and the sheaths are spindle-like and swollen.

The chief characteristics are the small size and the short, ovoid, spike-like panicle which when bent over the finger forms lobes along the outer edge like the Purple-stem Cat's tail.

It is distributed intermittently throughout Europe, growing chiefly in Denmark, Sweden and Norway, and in the western and southern parts of the continent. It is a pioneer plant of non-fertile sandy soils and is found round coasts, on sand dunes and beside certain rivers on poor, uncultivated soils. It is tolerant of drought, high salt concentrations and soils rich in lime. It cannot be used for grazing because it has shallow roots and is easily pulled up by sheep and cattle. From the aesthetic point of view it contributes nothing to the appearance of the landscape, not even improving occasional barren spots.

a) habit of the flowering plant with swollen basal part of stem
b) the same plant after it has dried
c) detail of spikelet

b   c   a

Smaller Cat's-tail

Phleum bertolonii DC.   Poaceae

The Smaller Cat's-tail is a slightly tufted perennial grass with stems which are tuberous at the base. The culms have a number of nodes and in summer bear spike-like panicles, about 6 millimetres (0·2 in.) wide, with short-awned spikelets. The leaf-blades are short, the ligules about 2 millimetres (0·08 in.) long.

The main distinguishing features are the tuberous culm bases, the low height — usually 40–50 centimetres (16–20 ins) — and the slender, cylindrical, spike-like panicles.

This grass grows from lowlands to foothills on dry soils and in open pine woods as well as on dry walls and in meadows and hedgerows. Its occurrence is closely associated with that of the common Timothy Grass, of which some authorities even regard it as a variety. However, as a forage plant it is of poorer quality than Timothy Grass. Leafy strains are highly valued for permanent pastures, particularly in England. Besides its value as a forage crop, newly bred strains are especially suitable for the formation of compact turf used in Britain for tennis courts and in Sweden for binding the soil on banks beside motorways to reduce erosion by wind and water. In all probability it will be used for the same purposes in other parts of Europe as well. Its resistance to frost and drought is fairly good and it is also tolerant of light shade.

a) vegetative part of the plant with bulbous basal internode
b) section of culm with spike-like panicle

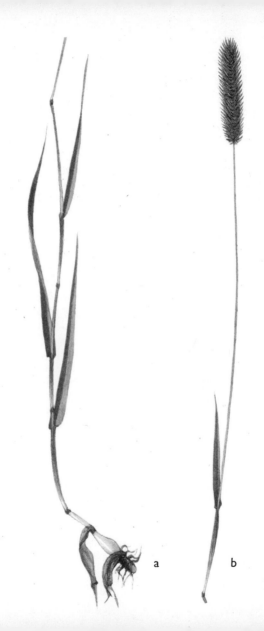

a   b

Meadow Fox-tail

Alopecurus pratensis L.   Poaceae

Meadow Fox-tail is a perennial, stoloniferous grass with tall erect culms. It starts into growth early in the spring and during the flowering period attains a height of up to 1 metre (39 ins). The leaf-sheaths are closely pressed to the stem, the ligules are 4 millimetres (0·15 in.) long and the blades are somewhat rough on the upper surface. The inflorescence is a dense, spike-like panicle with long-awned spikelets, which can be easily pulled off the stem. The glumes are hairy.

Meadow Fox-tail is an important cultivated meadow grass throughout all Europe. It does well in moist situations and is suitable even for boggy meadows where as a rule only weed grasses thrive. Its early growth provides an early harvest of a large quantity of quality fodder, the only drawback being the long awns of the inflorescence. It responds well to fertilizing. It is also a good follow-on grass in two- and three-crop meadows. However, it is not suitable for grazing because it is too tall and has poor powers of regeneration when trampled. When it occurs naturally on river, stream and pond margins, on roadsides, in parks and gardens, Meadow Fox-tail is a tall-growing species which is particularly effective in early spring.

a) the plant's habit
b) culm with flowering spike-like panicle
c) detail of awned spikelet

a   c   b

Slender Fox-tail or Black Twitch

Alopecurus myosuroides HUDS.   Poaceae

Slender Fox-tail is a tufted, fresh to greyish green annual grass. The culms are erect or bent at the basal node. It flowers from spring until autumn. The inflorescence is a tapering, awned, spike-like panicle. The leaf-sheaths are somewhat swollen, the blades are broad at the base and sharply pointed at the tip. The ligules are about 5 millimetres (0·2 in.) long and blunt.

The slender, 4–12 centimetre (1·5–5 in.) long, cylindrical, spike-like panicle narrowing at both ends and the roughness of the culm beneath the inflorescence are the main distinguishing characteristics.

This grass is distributed intermittently throughout Europe (chiefly in the south) and in western Asia, and has been introduced to North America and New Zealand. It has no special requirements and often grows on roadsides. In Europe it is a common weed found with cereal, rape and other crops, and in the southern regions it also occurs in vineyards. It is difficult to eradicate by the usual methods and proves a problem even for modern agriculture. It can, however, be used to good advantage as food for stock and if it grows to a height of 40–50 centimetres (16–20 ins) will give ample yields, but the long awns of the inflorescence can irritate the lining of the digestive tract, particularly in young cattle. Aesthetically, Slender Fox-tail is particularly welcome in dry southern regions where its long period of growth from early spring till autumn provides a continual green cover.

a) vegetative part of the plant
b) section of culm with spike-like panicle

a   b

Marsh Fox-tail

Alopecurus geniculatus L.   Poaceae

Marsh Fox-tail is a greyish green perennial grass with rooting shoots ascending from a bent basal node. It flowers the whole summer long. The inflorescence is a cylindrical, spike-like panicle, 5 centimetres (2 ins) long. The leaf-sheaths are slightly inflated, the blades are rough on the upper side and the ligules are long and blunt.

The chief features are the short-awned, cylindrical, spike-like panicles, blunt at both ends. The anthers are yellow during the flowering period, later turning brown. The entire plant and particularly the leaf-blades are covered with a greyish blue bloom.

This grass is a common weed throughout most of Europe, except in the south-eastern parts. It grows just as well on low as on high ground but requires a fair amount of moisture and thrives best in muddy places, damp meadows and pastures. It forms very loose growths which are generally no higher than 20–30 centimetres (8–12 ins) but occasionally the culms may grow to a height of 1 metre (39 ins). It is not very tolerant of competition from other grasses and generally occurs as a prostrate grass in marshy places, along river and pond margins. As fodder it is not very productive but on the other hand remains soft the whole year. As in other species of fox-tail, the awns are a disadvantage. Its value in the country-side rests in its lovely colouring and the ability to form a grass cover in muddy places and those exposed to heavy traffic so that it improves localities suffering from industrial blight.

> a) habit of the plant with shoots rooting at the nodes
> b) the same plant when dry
> c) detail of spikelet

a

b

c

Marram Grass

Ammophila arenaria (L.) LINK.   Poaceae

Marram Grass is a coastal perennial which forms culms up to 120 centimetres (48 ins) long in May and June. These are terminated by dense, cylindrical, spike-like panicles coloured greyish green and measuring as much as 20 centimentres (8 ins) in length. The leaves are large, often inrolled, the ligules extremely long and pointed and forked at the tip.

Distinguishing features are the formation of a dense greyish green cover, stout culms, cylindrical, awnless, spike-like panicles with one-flowered spikelets on silvery haired stalks, and long, pointed ligules.

This grass is widespread along the coasts of Europe, with the exception of Rumania. It tolerates high concentrations of salt and with its stout, rapidly spreading rhizomes binds and consolidates drifting sands. For these reasons it has been widely planted on coastal sands where it assists the formation of dunes. It is valued as a pioneer plant which stands up well to extreme conditions of climate and soil. It is one of the typical sweet grasses of coastal dunes where, together with Lyme Grass and other coastal grasses, it defines the character of the landscape. Marram Grass is most widely distributed in the colder parts of Europe but does not extend into the arctic. From the aesthetic viewpoint it is a very valuable grass because it retains its greyish green colour throughout the entire growing season. It may be used for grazing only to a limited degree because it becomes indigestible when it begins to form ears.

a) vegetative part of the plant
b) culm with cylindrical spike-like panicle
c) detail of spikelet

a

c

b

Hare's-tail

Lagurus ovatus L.   Poaceae

Hare's-tail is a small, ornamental annual grass forming
scant tufts of ascending culms from May till July. The
leaf-sheaths are greatly swollen, the leaf-blades are short,
the ligules about 1 millimetre (0·04 in.) long. The inflorescence is a very attractive, dense, oblong-ovoid, spike-like
panicle about 3 centimetres (1.2 ins) long, with a velvety
whitish green cast, an effect produced by the awned,
soft-haired glumes. The lemma is shorter than the glume
and is narrowed into two teeth. The whole plant is
greyish green and softly hairy.

Recognizable characteristics are the hairy, spike-like
panicle resembling a hare's tail, the swollen upper leaf-
sheaths and the short leaf-blades.

Hare's-tail is a native of warm Mediterranean regions
from where it has spread to other sunny, sandy places.
Occasionally it occurs as a weed, but in recent years
it is being used increasingly as an ornamental annual
planted in small groups in bedding schemes, in open
spaces after spring bulbs have finished and in rock gardens. Because of its delicate habit it is best sown in a seed
mixture. Good companions are other annual grasses such
as *Hordeum jubatum, Coix lacryma-jobi* and *Panicum capillare.*
However, it requires shorter grasses as associates, no
higher than 50 centimetres (20 ins). Hare's-tail has no
agricultural value; on the contrary, the long awns and
the hairiness of the leaves and inflorescence are a drawback.

a) culm terminated by spike-like panicle
b) detail of flowering spikelet
c) detail of flower

c   a   b

Blue Sesleria or Blue Moor–grass

Sesleria albicans KIT. EX SCHULT   Poaceae

Blue Sesleria is an attractive, chalk-loving, densely tufted perennial grass which starts into growth in early spring and generally flowers from March to May. The culms are erect and usually 30—40 centimetres (12–16 ins) high and the leaves are a lovely greyish green. The ligules are very short and fringed with hairs. The terminal inflorescence is a bluish grey, ovate or cylindrical, spike-like panicle, about 3 centimetres (1·2 ins) long with two- to three-flowered spikelets.

The scale-like bracts at the base of the bluish grey, spike-like panicle, the dense tufts, and the narrow, whitish stripes on the margin of the leaf-blades are the main distinguishing marks.

Blue Sesleria is widespread throughout much of Europe though absent in Denmark, Holland, Portugal, Greece and Turkey. It is found on calcareous and stony soils and is common at lowland, foothill and mountain levels. It frequently occurs in woodland clearings, on cliffs and in marshy meadows.

It has a robust root system so that it binds soils, especially stony soils and mountain debris, and its presence is a sign of good, humus-rich, calcareous soils. It is not of any particular agricultural value though it would be advantageous to exploit its intensive early spring growth. It remains a fresh green throughout the year but is relatively tough and does not spread much. Its lovely blue inflorescences and compact, fresh-green tufts are an asset in the rock garden and low borders.

a) habit of the flowering plant
b) ligule
c) flowering spikelet

a

b

c

Sweet Vernal-grass

Anthoxanthum odoratum L.   Poaceae

Sweet Vernal-grass is a small, perennial grass coloured a fresh yellow-green. It forms dense tufts with numerous culms bearing very dense, terminal, spike-like panicles. This is one of the earliest of grasses, flowering as early as April. It is noted for its relatively high content of the sweet-smelling substance coumarin. The basal leaves are short, about 5 millimetres (0·2 in.) wide, and covered with long, upright hairs. The ligules are also hairy, 2 millimetres (0·08 in.) long and toothed. Both ligules and leaf-sheaths are often tinged with purple.

The typical distinguishing feature of this grass is the very compact panicle resembling a loose spike. In the early stages it is yellow-green, at maturity golden-yellow. Interesting from the biological point of view is that Sweet Vernal-grass differs from all other grasses in that it has two instead of three anthers.

It is widespread throughout Europe and in the temperate regions of the world, even though in many places such as Australia it is not native to the region.

It grows in sunny, dry or shady localities and does well on acidic soils poor in minerals. It is also abundant on old meadows and pastures as well as in woodland clearings.

The bitter-tasting coumarin affects digestion and is thus of some, though little importance. In small doses it stimulates the appetite, but in larger doses it is toxic since it reduces the coagulating properties of the blood.

a) vegetative part of the plant
b) section of culm with spike-like panicle
c) inflorescence and culm when dry
d) detail of one-flowered spikelet

a   d   c   b

Crested Hair-grass

Koeleria cristata (L.) PERS.   Poaceae

Crested Hair-grass is a perennial forming dense tufts of greyish green leaves and stiff, erect culms. These have very few leaves and are downy towards the inflorescence. The flowering period is from May till August. The inflorescence is a more or less contracted, slender panicle with glistening spikelets, often purplish.

Most noticeable characteristics are the narrow leaf-blades and hairy leaf-sheaths.

Crested Hair-grass is widely distributed in the warmer regions of Europe and occurs usually in the company of other grasses. It is common on grassy steppes, warm sandy soils, cliffs and woodland clearings and on calcareous soils it may also be found at higher levels. It is a very variable species but of little agricultural value for it develops few leaves, rapidly becomes tough and affords little in the way of fodder. However, the glistening, contracted panicles are attractive and like *K. glauca intermedia,* a decorative grass with characteristic sea-green leaves and culms, it is grown in borders for ornamental purposes together with other grasses. Another species, *K. pyramidata* (var. *albescens* is particularly attractive), grows on coastal sand dunes and similar places, where it also consolidates sands.

a) vegetative part of the plant
b) section of culm with contracted panicle

a   b

Mountain Melick

Melica nutans L.   Poaceae

Mountain Melick is a dark-green perennial grass, about 50 centimetres (20 ins) high. The culms are loosely clustered and topped in May to June by loose racemes of purplish spikelets. The one-sided, nodding inflorescence is very attractive. The leaf-sheaths are rough, the lower ones often purplish and the leaf-blades are slightly hairy above. The leaves remain green until late autumn and are distinguished by short, brownish ligules.

The chief distinguishing characteristics are the somewhat tufted habit and one-sided racemes made up of regularly spaced, awnless spikelets.

Mountain Melick is widespread throughout Europe except in the extreme north, and extends as far as Asia, including the Far East. It grows in lightly shaded, humus-rich localities, particularly in deciduous forests and thickets. It stands up well to drought and is common on both low and high ground. It belongs to the group of grasses that contain cyanogenic glycosides. In some localities it is harmful and even poisonous having a greater concentration of hydrocyanic acid, and therefore cannot be recommended as food for cattle. In natural grasslands it is sometimes grazed as a supplementary, poor, woodland fodder. Though it has no agricultural value it is a decorative feature of woodlands and because of its good growth in shady places it could be of value as an ornamental grass.

a) habit of the flowering plant
b) vegetative shoot growing from the rhizome
c) detail of leaf with short ligule

Wood Melick

Melica uniflora RETZ.   Poaceae

Wood Melick is a delicate, dark green perennial with long creeping rhizomes which give rise to loose tufts of slender, sparingly branched culms. It flowers in May till September. The terminal inflorescence is a panicle made up of slightly drooping, one-flowered, awnless spikelets, which are usually tinged with purple. The branches in the upper part of the panicles are short, those at the bottom are long. The ligules are short, irregularly toothed and of unusual shape, prolonged into a slender bristle on the side opposite the blade.

The most marked feature is the loose panicle with rough branches of unequal length bearing one-flowered spikelets.

Wood Melick is a common grass of shady places throughout the whole of Europe. It generally grows on acidic soils and having no special light requirements it is often found growing with Wood Meadow-grass in open woods and shaded parklands, where it forms an attractive loose carpet. For this reason it is valued as a grass for places where heavy shade makes it impossible to grow a continuous grass cover.

Wood Melick provides only a negligible amount of fodder, which contains cyanogenic glycosides that release toxic hydrocyanic acid during decomposition in the digestive tract of cattle, but it is an attractive-looking grass which remains green practically the whole year round.

a) vegetative shoot
b) culm with flowering panicle
c) detail of section of leaf with ligule

a

c

b

Heath Grass

Sieglingia decumbens (L.) BERNH.   Poaceae

Heath Grass is a loose-growing perennial with ascending or somewhat prostrate culms reaching a height of about 40 centimetres (16 ins). In summer it bears loose panicles of awnless spikelets which are less than 1 centimetre (0·4 in.) long. The spikelets have characteristic lemmas, short and three-toothed at the tip. The leaves are greyish green on the upper surface and a glistening, fresh green below. The blade is practically the same width throughout with an abruptly blunt tip. In place of the ligule there is a fringe of short, spreading hairs.

The loose, compact panicle of oval, multi-flowered spikelets often tinged with purple, the fringe of hairs in place of the ligule, and the strap-like leaf-blade with its characteristic keel are the chief distinguishing factors.

Heath Grass is widespread, though not abundant, throughout the whole of Europe and is found also in Asia and Africa. At higher levels it grows on poorer types of grassland, heaths and moorland, reaching up to the alpine belt in mountain regions, often in the company of Matgrass. It is tolerant of very acidic soils and grows well also in wet places. Having no special light requirements it also occurs in the partial shade of woodlands.

It is of no particular agricultural value but the lovely colour of the leaves and spikelets make Heath Grass an attractive component of natural grasslands.

a) habit of the plant
b) culm with panicle
c) detail of spikelet
d) dried culm with panicle

a c b

Early Hair-grass

Aira praecox L.   Poaceae

Early Hair-grass is one of the smallest and most delicate of European grasses. It is an annual that forms shallow-rooting tufts and flowers in early spring, usually in April, occasionally from May to June. The culms are erect, short – sometimes barely 5 centimetres (2 ins) high, on good soils about 10 centimetres (4 ins), rarely higher – and terminated by contracted panicles. These are 1–3 centimetres (0·4–1·2 in.) long and made up of minute spikelets coloured greenish at first, later brownish white. Each spikelet contains two awned flowers with the awns projecting from the tip. The glumes are keeled and the lemmas are furnished with an awn on the back, one-third above the base. The leaves are also very delicate and thread-like, with ligule about 2 millimetres (0·08 in.) long.

The outstanding characteristic is the small size of the whole plant.

Early Hair-grass is a grass of sandy and lime-deficient soils and is found on heaths, in barren places and on stone walls, being content with only the smallest amount of soil, which is an additional reason for its dwarf habit. It is known also to occur on coastal sand dunes, and is more common in central, northern and western Europe. It is of no agricultural value nor is it of much worth as an ornamental grass because of its small size, though its dwarf habit might prove worthwhile as a short-lived plant in flat dishes in well-lit miniature, Japanese-style gardens.

a) habit of the flowering plant
b) the same plant when dry
c) detail of spikelet

b   a   c

Silvery Hair-grass

Aira caryophyllea L.   Poaceae

Silvery Hair-grass is a small annual with delicate, slender culms growing to a height of 10 centimetres (4 ins), very occasionally 40 centimetres (16 ins), from May to June. The panicles are contracted at first but later very loose with widely spreading branches. The leaf-blades are short and narrowly linear, the ligules long and pointed.

It can be identified by the small height and the spreading panicle. The spikelets are very small, tinged with purple or yellow, and furnished with bent awns projecting from the tips. The whole plant gives the impression of a silvery grass.

Silvery Hair-grass grows throughout Europe except in the extreme north. It prefers sandy, lime-deficient places, growing equally well at low or high altitudes. It is found in waste dumps, alongside walls and on fallow land. A very attractive, delicate grass flowering continually from late summer till early autumn, Silvery Hair-grass makes a decorative miniature for rock gardens and borders after spring bulbs have finished flowering. It is very tolerant of drought and is particularly attractive against the rocks of a rock garden. As an ornamental, this grass deserves greater attention than it has so far received. The silvery panicles are lovely also in natural grasslands, particularly in summer when most grasses are dry.

a) habit of the flowering plant
b) the same plant when dry

b   a

Creeping Bent or Fiorin

Agrostis stolonifera L.   Poaceae

Creeping Bent is a perennial grass spreading by long stolons which root at the nodes. It forms tufts of ascending
culms which are terminated by pyramidal panicles.
These are wide open while in flower (June to July) but
contracted before and afterwards. The branches of the
panicle are rough. The leaf-blades are flat and slightly
rough, the ligules long and irregularly toothed.

It can be distinguished by the long stolons which help
to form a close turf, the long ligules and the panicles with
the densely clustered, small, purplish, awnless spikelets
at the tips of the branches.

Creeping Bent is an extremely variable grass notable
for great differences in size and varying resistance to
extreme climatic conditions. It is widespread throughout
Europe, growing in moist to wet places, and is a weed
that stands up well in competition with other cultivated
grasses. It occurs abundantly on coastal sands, in flooded
areas and near water, in damp ditches, damp woods and
damp gardens. However, the densely clustered stolons
rot easily. This grass tolerates slight shade and may form
a short ground cover, usually 20 centimetres (8 ins) high,
or may grow up to 1 metre (39 ins) in height, depending
on the locality. Several new varieties have now been bred
which are suitable for the formation of turf on sports
fields, golfing greens and heavily trampled lawns.

a) vegetative part of the plant with stolons
b) culm with panicle
c) section of leaf with ligule

a

c

b

Black Bent

Agrostis gigantea ROTH.   Poaceae

Of all the bents this is the most robust one. It spreads by short rhizomes which in early summer produce tall culms, often more than 1 metre (39 ins) high, terminated by large panicles composed of delicate one-flowered spikelets. The panicle is pyramidal and open only when in flower. The leaf-blades are broad and slightly rough on the upper surface, the ligules are 2 millimetres (0·08 in.) long and rounded with a toothed margin.

Characteristic are the short rhizomes, the stout erect culms, the rough leaf-blades, the rough branches of the panicles and the spikelets clustered at the tips of the branches. In natural grasslands it is widespread throughout Europe and as a cultivated grass is grown in most parts of the world.

Black Bent is a tall perennial grass which slowly becomes fibrous as it ages. It grows well in various situations, even on very wet and flooded soils. Because of its late summer growth it is valued as a meadow grass yielding a large quantity of good forage. It responds well to extra feeding and is therefore regularly included in seed mixtures for permanent pastures. Many cultivated varieties have been bred for this purpose. It is not a suitable ornamental grass for lawns, but in parklands and natural grasslands it creates a very attractive effect with its robust yet delicate growth. It is generally listed as a subspecies of *A. alba*, namely *A. alba gigantea*, or as *A. stolonifera gigantea*.

a) vegetative part of the plant
b) section of culm with panicle

a

b

Common Bent

Agrostis tenuis SIBTH.   Poaceae

Common Bent is a perennial grass with short, creeping rhizomes. It starts growing very early in spring but does not flower until late June and July, at which time the culms are 20–50 centimetres (8–20 ins) high (on poor soils even less, on rich soils almost as much as 1 metre (39 ins). The panicles are permanently open, the branches spreading out in all directions. The spikelets, clustered at the tips of the branches, are one-flowered, awnless and tinged with purple. The basal leaves as well as those on the culms are flat; the ligules are only about 2 millimetres (0·08 in.) long and collar-like.

The chief distinguishing features are the flat blades, with the panicles remaining open even when the seed is ripe, and the culm being rough towards the panicle. The branches of the panicle are smooth.

This grass is a common European species found in a wide variety of localities. It is much valued in mountain regions, where it grows in meadows, pastures and open woods on very moist, often peaty soils. In the lowlands it is regarded as a worthless weed. It is crowded out by other cultivated grasses in well-fertilized soils, especially if concentrations of lime are increased. As an ornamental grass it is useful in permanent lawns, in sports-field turf, on waysides and in parks. A number of cultivated varieties with different climatic requirements and rates of growth have been bred for these purposes.

a) vegetative part of the plant
b) the same part of the plant when dry
c) culm with panicle
d) detail of spikelet

a   b   c   d

Brown Bent

Agrostis canina L. ssp *montana* HARTM.   Poaceae

Brown Bent is a perennial grass that forms greyish green, leafy tufts. Its main growth period is in late summer. The leaf-blades are bristle-like, the ligules about 3 millimetres (0·1 in.) long, pointed. The delicate panicle of brownish spikelets is open and spread out in all directions only when in flower; later it is contracted. The spikelets are one-flowered and furnished with small bent awns.

Brown Bent can be distinguished by its delicate habit and formation of rhizomes, the silky, thin basal leaves, the brownish spikelets, the rough branches of the panicle and the fact that it is open only when in flower.

It is widespread throughout Europe, where it grows in swamps, peaty meadows and pastures, though it is also found on sandy, stony and dry soils. It responds well to the application of artifical fertilizers, after which it forms a fine, compact turf. It stands up well to treading and extreme variations in climate, for which reason it is highly valued as a cultivated ornamental grass and with other grasses of similar qualities is included in seed mixtures for lawns exposed to a great deal of wear and tear. It is very good also for sports-field turf. Though of practically no agricultural value it greatly improves the appearance of the landscape wherever it is sown. It is now being more frequently classed as a separate species, *A. coarctata*.

a) habit of the flowering plant
b) detail of the leaf with ligule

b   a

Velvet Bent

Agrostis canina L. ssp *canina* HARTM.   Poaceae

Velvet Bent is a greyish green perennial of delicate habit
that flowers all summer from June till August. It forms
dense tufts of delicate basal leaves, often bristle-like.
The panicles are open when in flower, the spikelets are
about 2 millimetres (0·08 in.) long, tinged with purple
and arranged singly on short pedicels. The lemma is
furnished with a short awn.

Peculiar to this grass are the fine, bristle-like ground
leaves, the 2-millimetre (0·08 in.) wide leaves on the
flower-bearing culms and the formation of rooting stolons.
The branches of the panicles are rough. The lower ones
are divided into about five smaller branches.

Velvet Bent is common and widespread throughout
Europe and other continents. It is of no agricultural
value but because of its tolerance of bad weather and its
good growth in summer and autumn it does improve the
appearance of the landscape. With its creeping leafy
stolons and large quantity of soft leaves it quickly
covers areas where other grasses do not thrive. It is
found in peat moors and heaths, tolerates very wet and
acidic soils and grows well even in mineral deficient soils,
for which it is highly valued in western Europe and the
United States. It is propagated by means of the very
small seeds, and in some cultivated varieties also by division of the tufts. These are useful for golf greens and
close turf.

a) vegetative part of the plant
b) culm with panicle
c) detail of spikelet showing the awn on the lemma

c

b

a

Bristle-leaved Bent or Bristle Agrostis

Agrostis setacea CURT   Poaceae

Bristle-leaved Bent is a small perennial 20–60 centimetres
(8–24 ins) high, depending on the locality, with numerous
slender vegetative shoots. The culms are erect and in late
summer, usually from July to August, are terminated by
fine panicles made up of one-flowered, awned spikelets
tinged with purple. The blades of the leaves on the flower-
bearing culms are bristle-like. The ligules are about
3 millimetres (0·1 in.) long and pointed.

The main identifying feature is the grey to brown,
somewhat glistening sheaths of the basal leaves. This is
a very short, fine grass that grows in open, sunny grasslands and is a common component of grass communities
growing on roadsides. It is often found in places rich in
humus but grows also on stony ground and in rocky places. It thrives in low-lying areas as well as in the mountains, where it develops best, and is found even above the
tree line. It is not cultivated for agricultural purposes
but on waste land where it covers muddy and trampled
places it may serve as an occasional food plant. It is of
great value in the landscape because of its small habit
and late summer growth and is also noteworthy as an
ornamental garden grass. The inflorescence is often
dwarfed.

a) habit of the plant with panicle after flowering
b) culm with flowering panicle
c) detail of flowering one-flowered spikelet

a   c   b

Reed Canary-grass or Reed Grass

Phalaris arundinacea L.   Poaceae

Reed Canary-grass is one of Europe's most robust grass-es growing to a height of 2 metres (78 ins) where condi-tions are good. The rhizomes are stout, the culms stiff and erect, some terminated by large panicles in June and July. These are yellowish or greenish, often with a red-dish tinge; the spikelets are one-flowered and awnless. The leaf-blades are large and wide, edged with white near the ligule, which is also large.

Distinguishing features are the robust habit, the long ligules – often more than 6 millimetres (0·2 in.) – and the terminal panicle. Reed Canary-grass is common and widespread in Europe. It grows in wet places, chiefly on the margins of rivers and ponds and on damp, heavy soils. It stands up well to the competition of other grasses in meadows and often forms large dense stands resembling reed beds. From the agricultural point of view it is a plant of great possibilities and much value, being rich in pro-teins and yielding a large amount of fodder. It also has good powers of regeneration after cutting and is perennial; in fact, one day it may be even more important than Lucerne. Experiments in America have confirmed these findings on several occasions. However, ample watering is required for successful growth. Reed Canary-grass rapidly becomes fibrous during the flowering period and can be fed to cattle only after being processed for silage.

a) section of vegetative stem
b) stem with dried panicle
c) detail of flowering spikelet

a   c   b

Ribbon Grass

Phalaris arundinacea var. *picta* L.   Poaceae

Ribbon Grass is a perennial distinguished by its striped green and white leaf-blades. The leaves, striped lengthwise, grow from the creeping rhizomes early in spring, often as early as April, reaching a height of about 50 centimetres (20 ins). The 50–70-centimetre-long (20–28 ins) culms appear in June and are terminated by panicles composed of one-flowered, awnless spikelets clustered in groups. The sheaths of the ground leaves are often tinged with red. The ligules are long, the leaf-blades wide.

The green and white striped leaves, together with the early spring growth, are the chief means of identification.

This grass is one of the varieties of Canary Reed-grass which tolerates both sunny and shady situations. In the wild, it grows in damp localities, particularly on the margins of ponds and water courses. It is very frost-resistant and is much more common at higher levels, where it is found up to 1 050 metres (4 920 ft) above sea level. It is often cultivated as an ornamental not only because of its variegated leaves but also for its very early growth, which makes it useful for planting close to late-growing thermophilous grasses such as *Miscanthus*. It dries up in summer but quickly renews itself when cut and remains fresh and green until the frost. It may be fed to cattle, mainly before flowering. It is a traditional grass in country gardens in Europe's foothill and mountain regions.

a) culm with typical striped leaves
b) the same culm when dry
c) basal part of plant with creeping rhizomes

Canary Grass

Phalaris canariensis L.   Poaceae

Canary Grass is an annual growing to a height of 30–80 centimetres (12–32 ins) and coloured a fresh green, often with a delicate greyish bloom. The root system is fairly weak. Some of the culms are terminated by flower heads, others are sterile. The leaf-sheaths are smooth and wrapped around the stem, the ligules short and membranous, the leaf-blades large and wide. The nodes are a distinctly lighter colour — greenish-white.

The main distinguishing features are the ovate, spike-like panicles composed of overlapping spikelets with distinctive, flat glumes striped dark green (two thicker marginal lines and two thinner ones).

Canary Grass, so called because it originally grew in the Canary Islands, is a native of the warm Mediterranean regions from where it has spread throughout Europe, except in the extreme northern parts, as well as to other continents. It is cultivated on arable land and often occurs as a weed. Growth is vigorous throughout the summer. The seeds are used as food for cage birds. Breeding experiments indicate that this thermophilous grass is also of value as forage, most highly prized being its rapid growth, leafiness, high yield and slowness to become fibrous. It is furthermore very decorative so that it is also useful as an ornamental.

a) culm with leaves
b) section of flowering plant
c) ovate panicle when dry
d) detail of leaf with ligule

110

Loose Silky-bent or Silky Apera

Apera spica-venti (L.) BEAUV.   Poaceae

Loose Silky-bent is an important annual weed that flowers
in early summer. The culms grow to a height of about
1 metre (39 ins). The panicles are much-branched and
open. The fine branches, spreading in all directions, are
often crooked and terminated by one-flowered, long-
awned spikelets. The glumes are lanceolate, rough on
the keels; the lemmas are bristle-like, rough, with awns
up to 10 millimetres (0·4 in.) long. The leaves are
narrow, flat and smooth; the ligules long and irregularly
toothed.

The chief identifying factors are the broadly open,
spreading panicles with one-flowered, awned spikelets
and the long membranous ligules.

A weed of cereal crops, this grass is widespread throughout most of Europe, growing best in light soils, arable
as well as sandy ones, at both low and high altitudes.
It is regarded as a very serious pest. A single plant produces as many as 12 000 viable seeds which are shed before
the cereal crops are harvested and distributed great
distances by the wind or farm machinery. Many seeds
germinate in the autumn and can be eradicated by plough-
ing up the land before sowing spring crops. Herbicides
are also used for this purpose.

Loose Silky-bent is of little value as food nor is it of
much ornamental worth, for though it might be a decorative plant as a solitary subject, it requires the company
of other grasses for growth.

a) vegetative part of the plant at cereal harvest time
b) panicle after flowering

a   b

Wavy Hair-grass

Deschampsia flexuosa (L.) TRIN.   Poaceae

Wavy Hair-grass is a small, loosely tufted perennial with deeply embedded rhizomes, flowering throughout the summer. The attractive purplish panicles, with glistening, purplish to brownish spikelets, are 10–15 centimetres (4–6 ins) long, open and very loose, but contracted before and after flowering. The leaves are long, fine and bristle-like, remaining green for a long time; the ligules are about 1 millimetre (0·04 in.) long; the leaf-sheaths are smooth and often reddish. The numerous culms are also smooth and glistening.

The chief distinguishing marks are the rough, jointed or bent branches of the panicle and the long, bristle-like, dark-green leaves.

Wavy Hair-grass is widespread throughout Europe except Albania. It is usually found in woodlands in light shade but also in damp places on heaths and is abundant in lowlands, foothills and mountains.

It is of little agricultural use, though in the wild it is occasionally grazed by cattle. Its presence curbs the growth of other grasses and is an indication that the soil is rather poor. Its advantage is that it remains green in winter when it is grazed by wild game and improves the look of the landscape. It is of value also as a decorative grass for shady places in parks, smaller gardens and rock gardens.

a) habit of the dry plant after flowering
b) culm with panicle in full flower
c) detail of bristle-like leaf with ligule

a   c   b

Tufted Hair-grass

Deschampsia caespitosa (L.) BEAUV.   Poaceae

Tufted Hair-grass is a robust, densely tufted perennial growing to a height of 1·5 metres (5 ft). The rich green leaves are prominently ribbed and heavily saturated with silicates. They are tougher than those of many sedges. The culms are tall and smooth, rough towards the panicle. The panicles are beautiful — large, with branches spreading in all directions and a great many small spikelets. These are 3–4 millimetres (0·1–0·12 in.) long, brownish or purplish and shining. Tufted Hair-grass flowers in June and July and continues until September.

The main characteristics are the flat, longitudinally ribbed leaf-blades, the prominent ligules up to 8 millimetres (0·3 in.) long, and the large, firm tussocks formed by the plant.

Tufted Hair-grass is an important European grass growing in damp meadows, pastures and any grassy area. It easily adapts to different environments and is very tolerant of wet and peaty soils. When supplied with extra feed the leaves grow more upright, standing up well to the competition of other meadow grasses. It grows just as well at low as at high altitudes and may even be found in lightly shaded places. It is of great ornamental value in natural grasslands as well as in parks and gardens, and is particularly noteworthy as a solitary grass which retains its lovely dark green leaves throughout the winter. In botanical literature it is often classified as *Aira caespitosa*.

a) vegetative part of the plant
b) panicle
c) detail of leaf with ligule

a   c   b

Wood Small-reed or Bush Grass

Calamagrostis epigeios (L.) ROTH   Poaceae

Wood Small-reed is a robust, greyish green perennial grass with stiff, hard culms that are rough towards the panicle. It flowers in summer. The panicles are attractive, dense and clustered. The leaves and leaf-sheaths are rough, the blades often rolled, and the ligules are up to 7 millimetres (0·28 in.) long, blunt and irregularly toothed.

The chief distinguishing features are the robust, upright culms terminated by panicles which are open when in flower but compact afterwards. Characteristic of the flowering panicles are the yellowish orange to brownish anthers. The one-flowered spikelets are hairy and short-awned.

Wood Small-reed is widespread throughout most of Europe and often forms a dense cover in dry places, thickets, forest edges and sands, as well as on the margins of ponds and streams. In shady situations it usually does not flower. It thrives both in lowland and hilly regions.

It is not a good food for stock as its tissues become saturated with silicic acid during growth. It is of some value in binding drifting sands and also quite ornamental, even though it soon dries in summer. On a sunny day the glowing golden masses of this grass are reminiscent of prairie grasses. The genus *Calamagrostis* is very large and in Europe there are many species of similar appearance and value.

a) vegetative part of the plant
b) flowering panicle
c) detail of spikelet

a

c

b

Annual Meadow-grass

Poa annua L.   Poaceae

Annual Meadow-grass is a small annual, occasionally a biennial or short-lived perennial grass, coloured pale green to moss green. It usually grows to a height of 20–30 centimetres (8–12 ins) and its rapid growth and development are unrivalled by any other grass on the Continent. The period from germination to maturation of the seed takes less than two months and thus two to three generations a year are not at all unusual.

Characteristic features are the delicate, slightly spreading panicles of awnless, multi-flowered spikelets, usually on paired branches at the base of the inflorescence. The leaf-blades are short and blunt-tipped; the ligules are 2–3 millimetres (0·08–0·1 in.) long and collar-like.

This is one of the earliest spring grasses and rapidly forms a continuous, short grass cover. Nevertheless, it is not very welcome in grasslands in drier localities because of the rapid ripening of the seeds and its tendency to dry in periods of drought. It is regarded as a weed in gardens but valued in pastures, particularly around drinking pools, because it spreads rapidly and keeps the ground from becoming muddy. It is not suitable for grazing and hay production because it has a shallow root system and is easily torn up. On damp and fertile soils it remains a nice, fresh green practically all the time and flowers throughout the year.

Annual Meadow-grass is a true cosmopolitan, ranging from sea level to high mountain altitudes.

a) tuft of grass with flowering panicles
b) multi-flowered, awnless spikelet

a

b

Smooth Meadow-grass

Poa pratensis L.   Poaceae

This is the grass that gave the whole family its name Poaceae. Its palatability, softness and nourishment have caused it to be dubbed the bread of grasses.

It can be recognized by its rich, fresh green colour and also during the flowering period, from May till August, by the usually five-flowered, 5-millimetre-long (0·2 in.) spikelets. The spikelets are compressed and always awnless. The leaf-blades are flat, sometimes folded, 3–4 millimetres (0·1–0·12 in.) wide, and the ligules are very short and blunt. The leaf-blade of the topmost leaf next to the panicle is shorter than the sheath.

Smooth Meadow-grass is a very early species and very long-lived. It has no special requirements, tolerating damp as well as occasional drought, growing well on light as well as heavy soils, in lowlands as well as in the mountains. However, it does need ample light and is therefore found in meadows and pastures, and also in open woodlands.

It has a worldwide distribution and breeding has produced many forms with varying characteristics. The very short, thickly growing forms, reaching a height of several centimetres only, are good for lawns and sports fields, whereas the taller forms up to 1 metre (39 ins) high, are an important component of meadows. In pastures Smooth Meadow-grass is regarded as one of the most important of grasses responding well to large doses of fertilizer.

a) vegetative part of the plant
b) culm with panicle
c) detail of multi-flowered spikele during the flowering period

a

b

c

Narrow-leaved Meadow-grass

Poa angustifolia L.   Poaceae

Unlike the Smooth Meadow-grass, which is a cultivated species, the Narrow-leaved Meadow-grass is a grass of natural communities, chiefly grasslands, open woodlands, banks, gravelly soils and stony debris. It is far from such good quality as the cultivated Smooth Meadow-grass, nor is it so productive, and is less variable. In natural localities it grows to a height of about 70 centimetres (28 ins).

This grass is an example of the great variety exhibited by the Meadow-grasses, the width of the leaves being one of their important characteristics. In appearance, it is not very different from the Smooth Meadow-grass but the lower leaf-blades are rolled and bristle-like, indicating its greater resistance to drought. Some authorities regard it as a subspecies of Smooth Meadow-grass, giving it the name *Poa pratensis angustifolia* (L.) GAUD.

The roots of this grass rapidly penetrate to the deeper layers of soil but not nearly as deep nor as fast as some grasses, for instance, Upright Brome. Growth is both intravaginal and extravaginal, so that it rapidly forms a continuous grass cover, usurping the soil for its own growth and development. That is the reason why even in natural grasslands it is so hardy and persistent and in drier conditions on open grasslands it proves better than Smooth Meadow-grass. Like the latter, it produces extremely small seeds, about 4500 equalling 1 kilogram (2·2 lbs) in weight.

a) ground section of the plant with vegetative shoots
b) section of stem with panicle

a

b

Rough Meadow-grass

Poa trivialis L.   Poaceae

Rough Meadow-grass is a small, loosely tufted perennial, often with the lower part of the stems tinged with purple. It can be readily recognized by the tufted habit and erect culms, which frequently root at the nodes. The culms are rough towards the panicle. The blade of the uppermost leaves is shorter than the sheath with a ligule up to 8 millimetres (0·32 in.) long. The panicles are pyramidal, loose and regular. The branches are rough, the spikelets awnless.

Rough Meadow-grass has no special climatic or soil requirements and is therefore widely distributed. It is a native of northern and central Europe and Siberia and is widespread in North and South America as well as Australia, where it was introduced as a cultivated grass. It is generally found in grassy places, by waysides and in ditches, also in woodland clearings and unshaded marginal thickets.

This is an attractive grass that adds to the appearance of all natural localities wherever it occurs. The white form *P. trivialis* var *albomarginatis* was used for ornamental purposes in the nineteenth century.

a) vegetative part of the plant
b) section of culm with panicle
c) section of leaf with characteristic long ligule

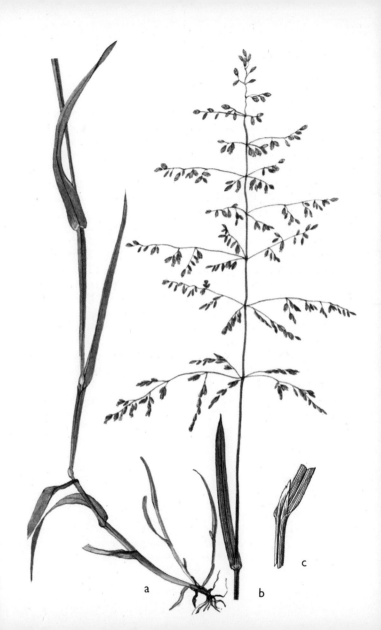

a   b   c

Wood Meadow-grass

Poa nemoralis L.   Poaceae

Wood Meadow-grass is a loosely tufted, rich green perennial, distinguished by extravaginal growth. Because it is tolerant of shade it is found chiefly in hornbeam and beech woods, on flat land and banks (together with melicks, wood millet and bromes), as well as in parks. It is widely distributed throughout Europe but because of its shallow roots it does not tolerate lengthy periods of drought and this makes it unsuitable for grazing.

In natural localities it can be recognized by its dark colour, loose growth and spreading upper leaves. The panicles are loose, slightly spreading, and often somewhat pendent at the top. The spikelets are very fine and appear to be one-flowered so that the amateur often mistakes this grass for bents. As a rule they are three- to five-flowered with awnless glumes and lemmas.

Recognition aids are the short, almost noticeable ligules and the long blades of the upper leaves. The leaves of this grass show marked variation in anatomical structure, according to differences in its habitat, but as a rule they are fine and thin.

The greatest advantage of this grass is its low light requirements. That is why it is recommended for partially shaded and shady places, particularly in older parks and woodlands.

a) basal part of culms
b) culm with flowering panicle and jutting leaves
c) junction of leaf-sheath and blade

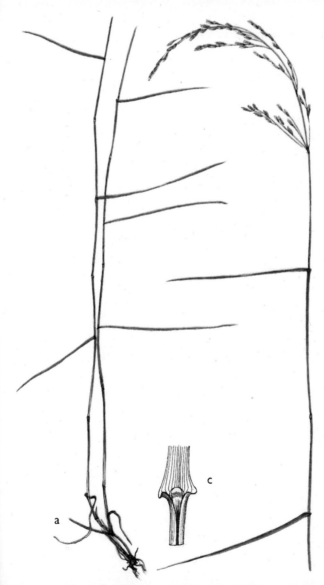

Flattened Meadow-grass

Poa compressa L.   Poaceae

Flattened Meadow-grass is a shorter, greyish green grass
growing to a height of 40 centimetres (16 ins.) The culms
are prostrate and bent at the base, often rooting, the
upper part upright and with short leaves. The leaf-
sheaths are compressed (like the culms) and open almost
to the base. The blades are about 5 millimetres (0·2 in.)
wide, pointed and slightly rough on the upper surface.
The inflorescence is a compact, partially one-sided panicle
with short branches bearing multi-flowered, purplish to
brownish, awnless spikelets. The flowering period is in
full summer, usually in July. This is a characteristic
wild grass of stony and dry localities. It grows along
waysides, beside pavements, in forest margins as well as
on dry walls, between stones and wherever there is
a marked lack of water.

It is easily recognized by the flattened culms which
are ellipsoidal in cross-section and so cannot be readily
twirled between the fingers. This has given the grass its
name — Flattened Meadow-grass. It can also be recognized by the short, firm branches of the panicle, which
are angular, rough and often brownish.

It is of no value in Europe but is of some worth on the
dry soils of infertile regions in North America. However,
it soon becomes fibrous and cattle will graze only the
rooting ground shoots. Its advantage is its ability to
withstand trampling.

a) flowering plant
b) habit of the plant after flowering
c) cross-section of flattened culm (enlarged)

130

a   c   b

Fern Grass

Catapodium rigidum (L.) C. E. HUBBARD   Poaceae

Fern Grass is a small or dwarf annual grass which sometimes overwinters. Its development is very rapid and thus
it is a short-lived species. It usually grows to a height of
about 10 centimetres (4 ins) but at times it forms a cover
only 3 centimetres (1·2 ins) high, at other times as much
as 20 centimetres (8 ins) high. It has short underground
stems which produce both vegetative and flower-bearing
shoots. The leaf-blades are long, often reaching above
the panicle. The small panicles are more or less contracted and composed of multi-flowered spikelets about 5 millimetres (0·2 in.) long.

The chief distinguishing characteristics are the rough
margins of the leaf-blades, their greyish green colour and
the low height of the flower-bearing culms topped by
small panicles. Whole plants are often reddish. They
grow in dry places, on walls, cliffs and between stones. Pro-
pagation is by the seeds, which ripen from June till
September.

Fern Grass is locally distributed throughout western
and southern Europe but it is not found in the Netherlands. It is of no agricultural value because it is small,
has very shallow roots, dries quickly and is ignored by
grazing animals. However, it is an attractive species
which may look decorative when planted in small groups
in the garden. Since it stands up well to being trodden
on it may be planted between the stones of garden steps
and dry walls. In botanical literature it is classified
also as *Scleropoa rigida*.

       a) flowering plant
       b) the same plant after flowering

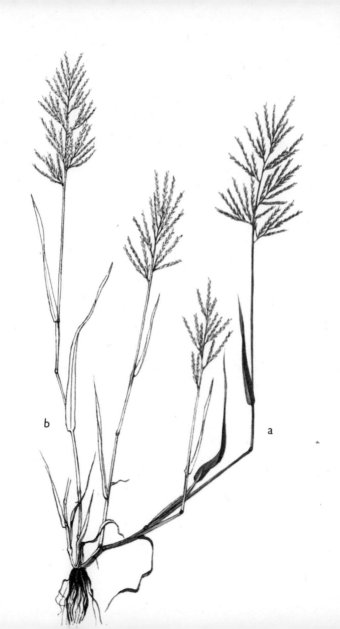

b   a

Reflexed Salt-marsh-grass or Reflexed Poa

Puccinellia distans (L.) PARL.   Poaceae

The Reflexed Salt-marsh-grass is a tufted perennial coloured greyish green and flowering from late spring until autumn. The inflorescence is a spreading, fairly small panicle. The branches of the panicle are rough, the spikelets purplish, usually five-flowered and awnless, so that they resemble meadow-grass. The stigma is feathery, as in most grasses, and seated on the ovary without a style.

It is recognizable by the very short pedicels of the spikelets and the leaf-sheaths which are open to the base.

The Reflexed Salt-marsh-grass is distributed throughout Europe, chiefly in the warmer regions, and in North America. It may be absent from some places, but elsewhere it covers large areas. It is a salt-loving species and is common on sandy and stony soils near the sea, on inland salt flats, as well as on waste land and rubbish tips. It is also found at higher altitudes and in mountain valleys up to 1 000 metres (3 280 ft) above sea level. It is of little agricultural worth for it produces a low yield but if well fertilized it forms a fairly dense cover and the food value is quite high prior to flowering. Animals are fond of it both as a pasture grass and as hay. It is a very decorative grass and can be used ornamentally as a solitary subject in gardens with poor and salty soils. In botanical literature it is often classed as *Glyceria distans*.

a) habit of the flowering plant
b) spikelet
c) section of leaf with ligule

c   a   b

Common Salt-marsh-grass or Sea Poa

Puccinellia maritima (HUDS.) PARL.　　　　　　　Poaceae

The Common Salt-marsh-grass is a greyish green perennial with ascending culms often rooting at the nodes. It
grows to a height of about 70 centimetres (28 ins) and
flowers from June till September. The inflorescence is
a panicle with longish, elliptical spikelets on short pedicels. These are five- to nine-flowered, about 10 millimetres (0·4 in.) long, awnless, and often purplish.

The most notable characteristics are the multi-flowered,
awnless spikelets on short pedicels.

This grass is distributed throughout Europe and Green-
land, along the entire coast of the North and Baltic seas
and is also found in Asia and North America. It grows
on salt flats, coastal meadows and pastures. It is often
a member of coastal plant communities, where it is of
value as a sweet perennial grass which is readily eaten by
cattle both as pasture grass and hay. It is very resistant
to high salt concentrations and can be expected to be
used in breeding new species and varieties for cultivation
as forage crops on salty soils.

Like the Reflexed Salt-marsh-grass, it can be used for
ornamental purposes in sunny, dry localities. In botanical literature it is often listed as *Glyceria maritima* or
Sclerochloa maritima, sometimes also as *Festuca thalassica*.

a) vegetative part of the plant
b) section of stem with panicle
c) detail of spikelet

a

c

b

Reed Sweet-grass or Reed-grass

Glyceria maxima (HARTM.) HOLMB.   Poaceae

Reed Sweet-grass is a perennial of marshy or wet places, with yellowish-green leaves and culms. It usually grows to a height of 1 metre (39 ins) but specimens more than 2 metres (78 ins) high are not unusual. In damp soil it spreads by creeping rooting stolons which bear smooth, fleshy culms with slightly keeled leaves. In summer the culms develop rich panicles with branches spreading in all directions. The spikelets are small, purplish to brownish.

It can mainly be recognized by the numerous, awnless spikelets, about 5–7 millimetres (about 0·2 in.) long, borne in large, loose panicles. The ligules are usually short and blunt with several shallow indentations.

Reed Sweet-grass grows in damp situations, usually in still or slow-flowing water, in meadows and damp ditches. Its distribution embraces the whole of Europe except the Iberian peninsula. Its anatomical structure is adapted to aquatic conditions; the leaves have large, air-filled compartments. Like other species of *Glyceria* it forms very little hard sclerenchymatous tissue and is therefore readily eaten by cattle. It is often attacked by Smut (*Ustilago longissima*), which is poisonous. This, however, is eradicated by drying. In botanical literature this grass if often listed as *Glyceria aquatica* or *G. spectabilis.*

A decorative variety with variegated leaves striped green and pale yellow is often planted on the margins of garden pools.

a) vegetative part of the plant
b) section of culm with flowering panicle

a   b

Floating Sweet-grass or Flote-grass

Glyceria fluitans (L.) R. BR.   Poaceae

Floating Sweet-grass is an aquatic perennial coloured fresh green and spreading by long creeping stolons. The culms grow to a height of 50 –100 centimetres (20–40 ins) and in summer are terminated by panicles measuring up to 40 centimetres (16 ins) in length and composed of thinly spaced, awnless, multi-flowered spikelets. Of interest is the anatomical structure of the leaves. These have air-filled compartments which enable them to float in the water. Young leaves are folded and at the junction of the leaf-blade and sheath there is a long ligule split at the tip.

Characteristic features are the more or less one-sided panicles composed of oblong spikelets 15–30 millimetres (0·6-1·2 ins) long with pointed lemmas and sharply two-toothed paleas.

Floating Sweet-grass grows throughout Europe except in the extreme north and is also widespread in north-eastern America and North Africa. It also tolerates flowing water, where it forms long, floating leaves, or it may grow in muddy or marshy areas.

As the common name indicates, the seeds have a sweet-ish taste and are edible. Floating Sweet-grass is eagerly grazed by cattle because its leaves and culms are compara-tively soft, readily digested and do not become fibrous even in late summer. It tolerates partial as well as total shade and forms a dense cover, together with other aquatic and marsh grasses.

a) vegetative part of the plant with characteristic keeled leaves
b) one-sided panicle in flower
c) vegetative part of the plant after it has died

a

b

c

Plicate Sweet-grass

Glyceria plicata FRIES.   Poaceae

Plicate Sweet-grass is an aquatic perennial, coloured grey
or fresh green. It usually grows to a height of about
50 centimetres (20 ins) but on fertile soils can grow up to
1 metre (39 ins). Like most species of Sweet-grass it forms
stolons rooting at the nodes. The leaves are flat and somewhat rough, the ligules about 5 millimetres (0·2 in.)
long and irregularly but prominently toothed. It flowers
in the first half of summer. The panicles are feathery and
composed of rather few linear, oblong spikelets coloured
green or purplish.

The chief distinguishing characteristics are the leaves,
which are doubly folded when young, and the wavy to
toothed margins of the lemmas, which have seven nerves
or veins.

Plicate Sweet-grass grows in damp meadows, in still
and flowing water and in swampy places both on low
and high ground. It tolerates basic soils and yields large
quantities of fodder. It makes hay from boggy meadows
more palatable and is readily eaten by cattle. It contains
varying concentrations of cyanogenic glycosides, depending on the site, but the amounts are never large enough
to be toxic. As in other species of sweet-grass the seeds are
edible and have a sweet taste.

Very similar in appearance to Plicate Sweet-grass is
Glyceria nemoralis which crosses with the former to produce
hybrids and is even regarded by some authorities as a variety of Plicate Sweet-grass (*G. plicata* var. *nemoralis*).
However, it differs in its lemma having a smooth margin.

a) part of the plant with rooting base
b) flowering panicle
c) multi-flowered, awnless spikelet

a

b

c

Wood Millet

Milium effusum L.

Poaceae

Wood Millet is a fresh green perennial grass spreading by creeping stolons and flowering from May to July. The culms are about 1 metre (39 ins) high, the leaves hairless, the ligules 5 millimetres (0·2 in.) long. The panicles are very loose, with thin, somewhat pendent branches bearing small, ovate, one-flowered, awnless spikelets. The entire plant is hairless.

The main features are the loose, spreading panicles with long branches terminated by one-flowered, awnless spikelets.

Wood Millet is widespread throughout most of Europe, growing chiefly in woodlands in partial shade and shady places, generally in thickets, in damp parklands, and occurring at high altitutdes.

This damp-loving woodland grass is of low agricultural value, affording little in the way of food, for it forms loose, scattered tufts. It is grazed by wild game and only very occasionally by cattle. After flowering the whole plant becomes quite tough, but the concentration of cyanogenic glycosides in this grass is very low so that it cannot be classed as poisonous.

It is of greater value for ornamental purposes. Its strong growth in shady situations, handsome broad leaves and fresh colouring together with its decorative, loose panicles make it an ornament of woodlands. It has recently become the object of greater attention as a decorative grass for shady spots in parks and gardens.

a) vegetative part of the plant
b) panicle with typical outspreading branches
c) spikelet during flowering period

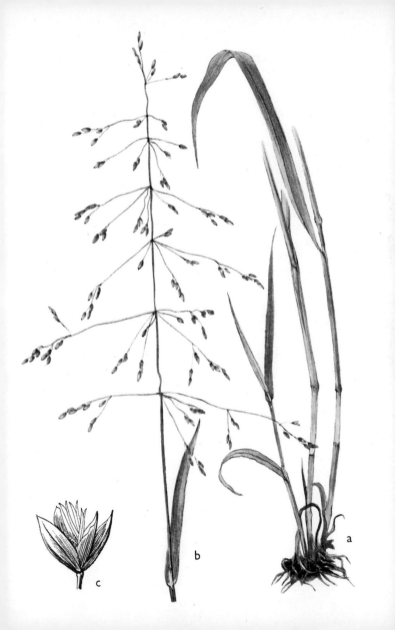

a

b

c

Common Quaking-grass

Briza media L.   Poaceae

Common Quaking-grass is a handsome, loosely tufted perennial growing to a height of 40–50 centimetres (16–20 ins). From May to August the short rhizomes bear slender, smooth culms terminated by open panicles with purplish, heart-shaped, multi-flowered spikelets about 5 millimetres (0·2 in.) long. The spikelets are awnless and very decorative. The leaves are rough on the margins; the ligules are short and blunt.

Easily recognizable are the heart-shaped, awnless spikelets on curved, hair-like pedicels.

Common Quaking-grass is distributed throughout the temperate regions of Europe and Asia up to altitudes of 2 000 metres (6 560 ft). In dense grasslands it does not stand up well to the competition of other grasses and it is becoming less widespread. It is readily grazed by cattle but because it produces very little leafage it is not of importance as an herbage plant. In natural grasslands it is a very ornamental element and it is also valued for this purpose.

Other attractive ornamental forms worth cultivating are *B. media* var. *lutescens* with yellowish spikelets and the Large Quaking-grass (*B. maxima*) with big, heart-shaped spikelets. Quaking-grasses are very attractive as solitary subjects in low borders and rock gardens.

a) vegetative part of the plant
b) panicle with typical, heart-shaped spikelets

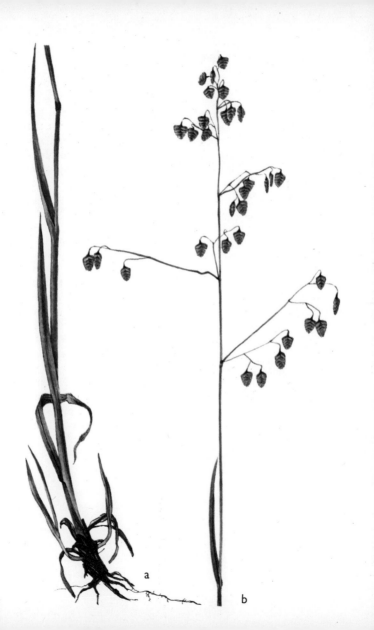

a

b

Purple Moor-grass

Molinia caerulea (L.) MOENCH.   Poaceae

Purple Moor-grass is a robust perennial growing to a
height of about 1 metre (39 ins). In late summer it produces slender, almost nodeless culms terminated at first
by contracted, later by open panicles of purplish, dark
spikelets. The spikelets are multi-flowered and awnless.
The leaves are slightly hairy and develop only on the
lower part of the culms, growing more densely on the
non-flowering shoots. The lower leaf-sheaths are thickened, the ligules are not developed. The leaf-blades are
erect, tough and coloured bluish green, with rough margins towards the tip.

The chief distinguishing features are the apparent
absence of nodes, as a result of which the culms are more
or less leafless, and the slender panicles, opening when in
flower, with short branches bearing purplish spikelets.

Purple Moor-grass is found both at low levels and
higher ground throughout Europe. It grows in damp
meadows with very low concentrations of nutrients and oxygen, on peat moors and fens, along water courses, on river
margins and marginal shallows. Its presence is an important indication of the poor condition of grasslands for
feeding purposes. The beautiful, dark-purple spikelets
arranged in loose panicles are very decorative in natural
localities which is why different varieties and species of
Moor-grass are grown for ornamental purposes, the most
beautiful being *M. caerulea* var. *variegata*.

a) tuft with vegetative parts of the plant
b) section of culm with panicle
c) detail of flowering spikelet

a

c

b

Cocksfoot

Dactylis glomerata L.   Poaceae

Cocksfoot is a densely tufted, bluish green perennial grass with short, unilaterally compressed vegetative shoots. It starts growing very early in spring and in May forms culms 1–1·5 metres (39–58 ins) high terminated by panicles bearing dense, one-sided masses of spikelets at the ends of the branches. The branches are fairly rough, those at the base of the panicles being longer and spreading. The leaves have a prominent keel; the ligules are 2–10 millimetres (0·08–0·4 in.) long with finely toothed or torn edges.

The chief distinguishing characteristics are the dense, one-sided masses of spikelets and the compressed vegetative shoots.

Cocksfoot is an important pasture grass distributed throughout Europe. In fact, having no special food or site requirements it is used universally in practically all continents, its great advantages being its early appearance, large size, and good growth in pasture and meadowlands as well as in field monocultures. It also does well in partial shade. Cocksfoot is traditionally regarded as one of the chief components of the so-called tough horse hay. The hardening of the leaves and culms, which occurs when the ears begin to form, is caused by silicon dioxide being deposited on the plant surface. This encrustation on the epidermis of the leaves and culms may cause irritation to the lining of the digestive tract of cattle.

Breeding and selection has yielded many productive varieties with various requirements for good growth and development.

a) vegetative part of the plant
b) flowering panicle
c) flowering spikelet

a   c   b

Yorkshire Fog

Holcus lanatus L.   Poaceae

Yorkshire Fog is a densely tufted, greyish green perennial grass with erect culms. The nodes and leaf-sheaths have soft hairs. The panicles flower throughout the summer and are distinguished by their pale purplish to pinkish colouring. The spikelets are two to three-flowered, about 4 millimetres (0·15 in.) long, and furnished with a minute awn.

Most recognizable characteristics are the tufts of culms thickly covered with soft, whitish hairs, the purplish spikelets and the panicles which are closed at first, opening when in flower, and triangular in outline.

Yorkshire Fog is a very common grass found throughout Europe. It grows in meadows, pastures and woodlands. It is abundant in lowlands, at higher levels and in mountains too. It is regarded as a weed in meadows and pastures even though when young it is readily eaten by cattle, both as a pasture grass and hay. The colouring of the culms and leaves and the delicate pink of the feathery spikelets make it a particularly decorative grass and an ornament in all places where it occurs. Another advantage of this grass is that the leaves remain green a long time so that it may also be used as a medium-sized ornamental, tufted grass for low borders in the garden.

a) basal part of the plant
b) section of culm with flowering panicle
c) flowering spikelet

a

c

b

Creeping Soft-grass

Holcus mollis L.   Poaceae

Creeping Soft-grass is a somewhat greyish perennial with creeping rhizomes forming shoots which bear culms terminated by flowering panicles in June and July. The panicles are composed of whitish spikelets borne on slender branches. The leaves and culms are generally smooth; only occasionally they have soft hairs.

The chief distinguishing marks are the panicles with whitish, small-awned spikelets and the nodes with long, reflexed hairs. Also characteristic is its habit of growing from creeping shoots so that it does not form tufts.

Creeping Soft-grass is found in western and central Europe, generally on high ground up towards the mountains. It forms loose growths in grassy places on damp and rather acid soils, and is found in pastures and on poor meadowlands, as well as in woodland clearings and fallow land. It is an extremely variable species. It is regarded as an unpleasant weed for its presence generally results in low yields, but it is hard to eradicate because of its good spreading powers. It is not so decorative as Yorkshire Fog as it dries fairly rapidly and even when in flower has a dull whitish hue, but because of its climatic tolerance and low soil requirements Creeping Soft-grass can be used ornamentally in gardens on poor soils.

a) basal part of the plant with characteristic hairy nodes
b) panicle beginning to flower
c) detail of flowering spikelet

a

b

c

Meadow Fescue

Festuca pratensis HUDS.   Poaceae

Meadow Fescue is a tufted perennial grass growing to a height of 1 metre (39 ins). The leaf-blades are ribbed on the upper side and glossy below. At the junction of the blade and leaf-sheath there is a barely noticeable ligule and two small auricles. It flowers in June. The panicles are contracted at first, later loose. The spikelets are more than 1 centimetre (0·4 in.) long and unlike most fescues are awnless. After flowering, often also while in flower, the spikelets are tinged darkish red or brownish.

Meadow Fescue is widespread throughout Europe and is commonly cultivated as a very productive and nourishing meadow and pasture grass. It grows well in meadows and all grassy places, even in woodlands if provided with sufficient light, and is found in lowlands as well as at higher altitudes. It is one of the most valuable of cultivated grasses, spreading readily during the hay season and afterwards and producing very little fibre. It forms a large root system so that it stands up well to drought but grows just as well in damper soils. Because it has no special soil requirements it may be found on loam, sand or clay soils. It stands up well to extremes in climate, particularly to dry frost and long-standing snow cover, and holds its own very well in competition with other grasses and broad-leaved species.

a) culm with basal rooting part of the plant
b) panicle of awnless spikelets
c) detail of leaf showing junction of blade and sheath

b

c   a

Tall Fescue

Festuca arundinacea SCHREB.   Poaceae

Tall Fescue is a robust, loosely tufted perennial grass about 1 metre (39 ins) high, though in fertile soils it grows to a height of more than 1.5 metres (58 ins). In appearance it resembles Meadow Fescue but its leaf margins are rough. It flowers from May till September. The panicles are loose and made up of multi-flowered, usually awnless or only short-awned spikelets.

The chief features to note are the smoothness of the culm towards the panicle and the rough branches of the panicle. The upper side as well as the margins of the leaf-blades are also rough. The small, narrow auricles are covered with soft hairs and so is the blade next to the junction.

Tall Fescue is found in lowlands as well as mountains throughout most of Europe and is tolerant of cool climates.It has a good rate of growth, but becomes fibrous fairly rapidly so that it is not as readily grazed by cattle as Meadow Fescue. Nevertheless it is worthy of note not only in agriculture for breeding and cross-breeding purposes but also in natural grasslands, for it is a vigorous species which because of its large root system is very resistant to unfavourable conditions such as drought, damp and frost. It is a very variable grass exhibiting marked differences according to its habitat. It requires further detailed study which will doubtless lead to the development of new varieties with excellent qualities as pasture grasses.

a) basal part of the plant with vegetative shoots
b) section of culm with panicle
c) part of leaf with auricles

a

c

b

Chewings Fescue

Festuca rubra L. ssp. *commutata* (GAUD.) ST YVES   Poaceae

Chewings Fescue is a densely tufted perennial grass about 50 centimetres (20 ins) high. It is distinguished by its bristle-like, very occasionally flat, basal leaves. From May till August it produces numerous culms with slender panicles, open only during the flowering period. The spikelets are small, often reddish and furnished with short or medium-long awns.

The most striking characteristics are the dense tufts with young shoots growing up within the leaf sheaths (intravaginal growth) and the three- to six-flowered spikelets. The basal leaves are nearly ovate in cross-section with seven vascular bundles, the leaves of the culm are V-shaped in cross-section or flat. On the inner side of the blade they are furrowed lengthwise and covered with fine hairs.

Chewings Fescue is widespread throughout Europe, growing under very harsh conditions usually from mountain foothills to sub-alpine altitudes. It is of great value in the wild because it binds soil even on steep slopes and thanks to its negligible requirements is a species which remains green both in dry summer weather and during frosts in winter. It is therefore one of the grasses that help to keep the landscape green without any special demands or care. It is propagated by means of seeds. In botanical literature it is often classified as *F. rubra fallax* or *F. rubra eu-rubra* var. *fallax*.

a) vegetative tuft with part of the rootstock
b) culm with panicle

b   a

Creeping or Red Fescue

Festuca rubra L. ssp *rubra*   Poaceae

Creeping Fescue is a loosely tufted grass with creeping rhizomes forming loose patches in many grass communities. In June and July it bears culms 50 centimetres (20 ins) high, terminated by flowering panicles which are more or less contracted in the upper part with a branch jutting out sideways at the base. The spikelets are usually reddish, four- to nine-flowered and short-awned. The basal leaves are generally bristle-like; those of the culm are flat or more usually rolled.

It can be recognized by the loose habit of the bristle-like leaves and the way in which the lowest branch of the flowering panicle juts out horizontally.

Creeping Fescue is very common throughout Europe. It is a very persistent grass and even in localities with insufficient humus and soil moisture it grows fairly well and seeds itself readily, producing a good yield of viable seeds which develop well from the beginning. Because of these traits Creeping Fescue is one of the most important grasses not only for meadow and pastureland but also for fine lawns, sports fields and similar areas. It will even grow on acidic and damp soils where other cultivated grasses do not thrive. In view of these advantages it has also been the subject of breeding and selection which has yielded various short and tall forms with differing rates of growth, depending on the uses to which the grass is put.

a) vegetative part of the plant
b) panicle with finger-like branch
c) multi-flowered, awned spikelet

162

a   c   b

Sheep's Fescue

Festuca ovina L.   Poaceae

Sheep's Fescue is a low perennial generally coloured greyish green, occasionally grass-green. In June, or even earlier, it bears up to 50-centimetre-high (20 ins), slender culms, slightly rough near the panicle. The leaves are cylindrical, hair- or bristle-like, tightly infolded so that in cross-section they practically form a circle. The ligules are extremely short. The spikelets are multi-flowered and short-awned.

The chief distinguishing factor is the length of the leaf-blade which is half as long as the sheath. The blade is rough and hairy near the tip.

Sheep's Fescue forms a densely tufted cover at low as well as high levels, particularly on acidic soils, and also tolerates slight shade. It is widespread throughout Europe, Asia and North America. Because of its fibrous nature it is of little value for grazing, being used for this purpose only on very poor soils. It is extremely variable and many varieties and subspecies have been described. None, however, is of any great agricultural value. Because it has no special soil or climatic requirements it is of importance for breeding purposes. It is not particularly decorative but it is biologically useful as a grass cover for poor soils because it forms loose spreads even in woodlands where other species do not flourish for lack of light.

a) habit of the flowering plant
b) detail of multi-flowered spikelet
c) cross-section of leaf with characteristic pattern of dark-coloured vascular bundles

a

c

b

Hard Fescue

Festuca longifolia THUILL.   Poaceae

Hard Fescue is a short, greenish, loosely tufted perennial flowering from May to June. The culms are about 10–40 centimetres (4–16 ins) high and terminated by small panicles of small, awned spikelets. The leaves are needle-shaped, fibrous and about 1 millimetre (0·04 in.) in diameter.

This grass can be identified by the multi-flowered spikelets with awns nearly as long as the lemmas. The spikelets are usually five-flowered, the pedicels short.

Hard Fescue has a scattered distribution throughout Europe, growing mainly in the warmer regions. It has no special requirements and can be grown practically everywhere, though it prefers poor, non-calcareous soils. It grows well on roadsides, sheep pastures, peat moors, in stony and sandy localities, tolerates trampling and treading and exhibits good powers of regeneration when grazed. Because of its habit, Hard Fescue may also be used for ornamental purposes. Just as suitable for rock gardens and low borders are those species of fescue that grow no higher than 10–20 centimetres (4–8 ins), chiefly *F. valesiaca, F. scoparia, F. glacialis* and *F. glauca.*

a) tuft with part of the root system
b) section of culm with panicle
c) multi-flowered, awned spikelet

a

b

c

Fine-leaved Sheep's Fescue

Festuca tenuifolia SIBTH.   Poaceae

Fine-leaved Sheep's Fescue is a small, densely tufted perennial growing to a height of 10–30 centimetres (4–12 ins) and flowering in June and July. The inflorescence is a panicle with short branches bearing small spikelets about 5 millimetres (0·2 in.) long, usually five-flowered and awnless. The leaves are thin, hair-like and rough towards the tips; the ligules are extremely short. These are also the most important characteristics of this grass.

Fine-leaved Sheep's Fescue is distributed chiefly in western Europe. It forms a large root system which renders it resistant to both drought and cold and enables it to grow on poor soils. If the mineral composition of the soil is favourable it is of great value as a turf-binder. It is also tolerant of acidic soils, has good powers of regeneration when grazed and trampled, and thrives even in mountains, particularly on lime-free soils. These traits make it a valuable pasture grass for sheep not only in Europe but elsewhere as well. In botanical literature it is often classified as *F. capillata*.

Because of their bluish colouring some species of fescue are also planted for ornamental purposes. These are chiefly *F. glauca*, *F. amethystina*, and *F. valesiaca*, which somewhat resemble the Fine-leaved Sheep's Fescue. Particularly outstanding is *F. amethystina* with its beautiful bluish colour and resistance to frost.

a) tuft with flowering culms
b) section of culm with panicle after it has died

Giant Fescue

Festuca gigantea (L.) VILL.   Poaceae

Giant Fescue is a loosely tufted, woodland perennial growing to a height of more than 1·5 metres (58 ins) and fully deserving its name 'giant'. It forms a loose cover and begins flowering in the second half of summer. The culms are tall and terminated by long panicles of awned spikelets. The panicles are somewhat spreading at first, later pendent. The leaves are often up to 2 centimetres (0·8 in.) wide with prominent auricles.

The distinguishing characteristics are the long, slender awns, two or three times longer than the lemmas, the wide leaves and the prominent auricles.

Giant Fescue is widespread at both low and high altitudes throughout most of Europe. It is found in shady places, particularly in woods and on the edges of woodlands and near thickets. It remains a fresh green even in dry summer weather.

It is regarded as a weed and can be grazed in woodlands only when young. It is of far greater value as an ornamental asset to the landscape due to its late flowering and green colour retained throughout the year. It can also be used in the garden, where its good growth in shade is also appreciated. No doubt the efforts of breeders will produce lovely new forms of this species which can be used to good effect in large parks and recreation woodlands outside cities.

a) vegetative part of the plant
b) section of culm with panicle
c) detail showing section of leaf with auricles

170

a

b c

Soft Brome

Bromus mollis L.   Poaceae

Soft Brome is an annual or, in mild climates, biennial grass coloured greyish green and forming tufts about 50 centimetres (20 ins) high. The whole plant has soft hairs. The more or less contracted panicle is composed of multi-flowered spikelets which are flattened, medium-long and furnished with awns. The ligules are short and collar-like, the leaf-sheaths entire.

The main recognition factors are the soft hairs covering the whole plant and the plump, short-awned spikelets. The lower branches of the panicle are shorter than the spikelets. Soft Brome flowers in May and June and forms an attractive greyish green cover. During the growth period it often acquires a purplish tint and may suddenly wither and die away.

Soft Brome is an important, thermophilous grass widespread in Europe and Asia. It frequently occurs on waste ground, roadsides, and around human dwellings.

When young, until it forms ears, it may be fed to all stock. After ears have formed it rapidly becomes tough, even though its fine hairy covering makes it seem like a soft grass. It does not tolerate lack of moisture and soon dries so that it is of no value for occasional grazing and detracts from the appearance of the areas where it occurs. Its presence in meadowlands is negligible but if harvested in time it can be used to good purpose in hay.

a) vegetative part of the plant with part of root system
b) section of culm with panicle
c) detail of leaf with ligule

a

b

c

Upright Brome

Zerna erecta (HUDS.) S. F. GRAY   Poaceae

Upright Brome is a tufted grass 60–70 centimetres
(24–28 ins) high, with many thin leaves, located primarily
on the lower part of the plant, smooth or slightly hairy
leaf-sheaths, and very short, collar-like ligules. The
margins of the blades are markedly hairy. The panicles
are upright, contracted and made up of awned spikelets
more than 2 centimetres (0·8 in.) long and often brownish. This grass can be distinguished from other bromes
by the upright panicles with their branches shorter than
the actual spikelets. Noteworthy is the fact that it does
not produce non-flowering stems; all the culms bear
panicles.
  Upright Brome grows in dry, grassy places and calcareous soils. It has a large root system and is therefore
drought-resistant. It needs ample sunlight but has no
special food requirements and so may be found on poor
soils. Widely distributed throughout Europe, particularly in the warmer regions, it occurs also in Asia and
Africa.
  Upright Brome contains large amounts of mineral
substances and proteins. The large, stiff leaves contain
hard, indigestible, sclerenchymous tissue, which is the
reason for the low quality of this grass. It is of much
greater value in binding soil and curbing erosion for it
forms a close turf.
  This grass was formerly known as *Bromus erectus*.

a) vegetative part of the plant with section of the root system
b) section of culm with panicle
c) section of leaf with characteristic tubular sheath and ligule

a

c

b

Barren Brome

Anisantha sterilis (L.) NEWSKI   Poaceae

Barren Brome is a drought-resistant annual, occasionally biennial grass of fairly rapid growth. It generally reaches a height of 30–100 centimetres (12–40 ins), flowers in May and June and quickly ripens. It seeds itself readily.

The chief distinguishing features are the loose panicles with long, drooping branches spreading in all directions and terminated by long-awned spikelets. Together with the awns, the spikelets measure more than 2 centimetres (0·8 in.) in length. When pressed between the fingers they appear to be barren – hence the plant's name. The entire plant is reddish to purplish, particularly during and after flowering. It looks very much like the Drooping Brome (*A. tectorum*), in which the culms are hairy near the panicle and the panicles dense and drooping to one side.

Barren Brome is widespread throughout most of Europe and Asia and has been introduced also into America. It generally grows near human dwellings, on rubbish tips, by roadsides, on railway banks, construction sites and waste ground.

It is a typical example of a grass with no agricultural or aesthetic value. On the contrary, it is often the cause of the untidy appearance of the places where it occurs. When young it can be used as occasional fodder, but later it is very harmful to stock because its hard culms and long awns damage the lining of the digestive tract.

It was formerly known as *Bromus sterilis*.

a) section of culm with typical panicle
b) detail showing part of the leaf and culm with ligule

a   b

Hairy or Wood Brome

Zerna ramosa (HUDS.) LINDM.   Poaceae

Hairy Brome is a robust, dark-green perennial grass growing to a height of 1·5 metres (58 ins). The flowering period begins in late June and lasts till August. The panicles are slightly pendent, contracted at first, later loose and open. The spikelets are more than 2 centimetres (0·8 in.) long and are furnished with long awns. The entire plant is hairy; the leaves are large with blades more than 1 centimetre (0·4 in.) wide. The leaf-sheaths are markedly hairy, the ligules prominent and toothed.

The most outstanding characteristics are the rough, open panicles of drooping spikelets with branches of the panicle arranged in pairs.

Hairy Brome is distributed throughout most of Europe except in the Netherlands, Portugal, Iceland, Finland and Albania. It is found also in central Asia and North Africa and was introduced into North America. In these parts the plant's late development and late onset of the flowering period are regarded as an advantage. Hairy Brome is an important grass of deciduous woodlands but grows also in parks and woodland clearings. It tolerates moderate shade and grows both on low and high ground. This robust woodland grass soon becomes tough and the loose and scattered tufts afford very little in the way of fresh herbage and hay. It is a handsome grass and until late summer improves the look of the landscape wherever it grows.

Botanically, it was formerly known as *Bromus ramosus*.

a) vegetative part of the plant
b) open, pendent panicle
c) detail of section of culm and leaf at the junction of the leaf-sheath and blade

a   c   b

Meadow Brome

Bromus commutatus SCHRAD.   Poaceae

Meadow Brome is an annual grass of medium height up to 90 centimetres (36 ins) high. The culms are erect and terminated by loose panicles of awned spikelets. The lower leaf-sheaths are entire and densely haired. The ligules are about 2 millimetres (0·08 in.) long. The spikelets are composed of a great number of florets, often as many as eight or eleven in a spikelet. They are coloured greyish green and later often become reddish.

Meadow Brome somewhat resembles Soft Brome, the chief distinction being the many florets in the spikelets and the open panicles, drooping after flowering. The awns on the spikelets are straight even when the seeds are ripe and practically all are of the same length. The flowering period is in May and June but occasional flowering specimens may be found as late as October.

Meadow Brome is widely distributed throughout Europe and occurs also in Africa. Alpine valleys up to altitudes of 1 200 metres (3 900 ft) mark the limits of its range but it does best in lowlands and foothills. .It is found on moist, loamy soils, moist fields, fallow and waste land, and is a serious weed of clover crops.

Only young plants, until they form ears, may be used for green fodder and hay. Later the culms become very tough and together with their awns are more of a disadvantage in fodder than otherwise. Meadow Brome is not of any great ornamental value in the landscape.

a) vegetative part of the plant
b) culm with panicle
c) detail of awned, multi-flowered spikelet

180

a

b

c

Squirrel-tail Fescue or Barren Fescue

Vulpia bromoides (L.) S. F. GRAY   Poaceae

Squirrel-tail Fescue is an annual or biennial grass 20 centimetres (8 ins) or more high, flowering from May till July. The panicles are compact, with small four- to six-flowered, purplish, awned spikelets. Most of the leaves are rolled. The ligules are barely visible and collar-like.

The chief distinguishing characteristic is the 10-centimetre-long (4 ins) panicle with its alternating branches. The awns are twice as long as the lemmas on which they are borne.

Squirrel-tail Fescue is distributed mainly in central Europe but its range extends as far as Sweden. It is also found in Asia and North and South Africa. It grows on sandy soils, generally in lowlands and foothills. In most places where it occurs it is not native but has been introduced. This grass tends to dry quickly and, like the annual barleys regarded as weeds, does not add to the attractiveness of the places where it occurs. It may thus be looked on as a somewhat negative element in the countryside, and one that is of no value because of its small foliage yield.

Other species of *Vulpia*, such as *V. myuros* and *V. ciliata*, may be found growing in similar situations to the Squirrel-tail Fescue. The first has panicles up to 20 centimetres (8 ins) long, the second has panicles with hairy awns and spikelets.

Vulpia was formerly included in the genus *Festuca* but is now classed as a separate genus.

a) vegetative part of the plant
b) section of culm with panicle
c) detail of spikelet

a   b   c

Common Reed

Phragmites communis TRIN.   Poaceae

The Common Reed is one of the most robust of European
grasses, growing to a height of up to 3 metres (117 ins)
in summer during the flowering period. The panicles
are large, often 30 centimetres (12 ins) or more in length,
and purplish with silvery hairs. The spikelets are about
1 centimetre (0·4 in.) long, multi-flowered, awnless, with
soft silvery hairs. The leaves are greyish green, the blades
large, the ligules replaced by a fringe of long, whitish
hairs. Another typical characteristic is the formation of
stout, very long rhizomes.

The Common Reed is widespread throughout most of
Europe, extending to Asia and North America. It grows
in places with fertile soil and ample moisture, such as
river deltas, stream, pond and lake margins, wet and muddy meadows and alder woodlands, often forming tall,
impenetrable masses. Because of its rapid development
it ranks first among grasses in the prodution of biomass.
Its greatest use is currently in industry, particularly the
building industry, as thatching, and in some countries
in the prodution of paper. It is of very little use as
fodder but is of great aesthetic value in giving distinction
to flat landscapes and enhancing the beauty of tracts of
water and water courses. It is also of value in park
landscaping, where use is made chiefly of the ornamental,
brightly coloured species.

a) section of rhizome
b) part of culm with panicle
c) detail of spikelet

a   b   c

Yellow Oat-grass

Trisetum flavescens (L.) P. BEAUV.   Poaceae

Yellow Oat-grass is a tufted, pale green to yellowish perennial which flowers from May to June. The culms are slender, ascending, and terminated by panicles composed of a large number of small, two- to four-flowered, awned spikelets. These are golden green at first, later a gleaming golden yellow. The leaves are delicate, the ligules short and irregularly toothed.

The main features are the tufts and the 5-millimetre-long (0·2 in.) spikelets with fine, roughly haired awns. Each single spikelet generally has three flowers, each with its own awn.

Yellow Oat-grass is distributed throughout Europe except in the extreme north and is also found in northern Africa, Asia Minor, the Far East and North America. It requires light, oxygen-rich, calcareous soils and flourishes at both low and high altitudes. In the mountains it grows far above the tree line and is resistant to frost, drought and wet conditions. One disadvantage of this grass is the awns which may injure the digestive tract of cattle, but it is frequently sown for fodder and grows in practically all European meadows and pastures. It is also used in grass breeding experiments to produce taller and more productive varieties. A great advantage of this species is its good rate of growth and repeated flowering even in autumn so that it can be harvested for hay more than once a year.

a) culm with basal rooting part
b) section of culm with panicle before flowering
c) detail of spikelet

a   b   c

Tall Oat-grass

Arrhenatherum elatius (L.) PRESL.   Poaceae

Tall Oat-grass is a perennial often more than 1·5 metres (58 ins) high which begins to flower in June. The panicles are closed at first, opening later. Open, flowering panicles may be seen even towards the end of the season. The spikelets are about 1 centimetre (0·4 in.) long, greenish, later yellowish or purplish, with typical, protruding, bent awns. The leaves are smooth or finely haired, the blades often up to 1 centimetre (0·4 in.) wide. The ligules are usually short and toothed.

The two-flowered spikelets, generally furnished with a single, bent awn, and the robust habit of growth are the distinctive features to look for.

Tall Oat-grass is distributed throughout Europe, growing in grassy places on fertile soils. Of rapid growth and with a great quantity of leaf it is commonly cultivated and sown as a meadow grass, but it does not tolerate frequent cutting and trampling. For this reason it is good only for meadows. It has not proved very successful as a single field crop because it has a slightly bitter taste and is not palatable to cattle.

In *A. elatius* var. *bulbosum* the basal parts of the culms are bulbous. It is a troublesome weed, unlike the cultivated species, but the same form with variegated leaves is decorative and used to good effect as a solitary grass in garden landscaping.

a) vegetative part of the plant
b) section of culm with panicle before flowering
c) detail of spikelet with bent awn

a   c   b

Meadow Oat-grass

Helictotrichon pratense (L.) PILGER   Poaceae

Meadow Oat-grass is a slightly greyish perennial that in late May or June bears stiff, erect culms which are rough near the panicle. During the flowering period the culms grow to a height of 50–80 centimetres (20–32 ins). The panicles are narrow with rough, erect branches. The spikelets are 2·5 centimetres (1 in.) long, three- to eight-flowered, and furnished with long, glistening, purple-spotted, bent awns. The spikelets are placed close above each other and some lean out slightly from the axis. The leaf-blades are short, flat and rough, with prominent auricles and ligules up to 5 millimetres (0·4 in.) long. The basal leaves are often more or less inrolled, and bristle-like.

The chief distinguishing characteristics are the flattened, bent awns, the smooth, lower leaf-sheaths, and the rough blades with thickened margin.

Meadow Oat-grass is locally distributed throughout Europe. It thrives particularly well in sunny situations and is very tolerant of drought, forming a component of dry grassy plains. It is a typical grass of poor calcareous soils, particularly those with low concentrations of nitrogen. The presence of this grass is characteristic of natural or untended grasslands. It has no agricultural or aesthetic value, but in view of its minimal food requirements it may be useful as a green cover in localities exposed to the sun with poor soil that tends to be very dry.

a) vegetative part of the plant
b) section of culm with panicle
c) detail of spikelet showing the ventral and dorsal sides

a

c

b

Hairy Oat-grass

Helictotrichon pubescens (HUDS.) PILGER   Poaceae

Hairy Oat-grass is a loosely tufted perennial with creeping stolons. In May and June it develops culms up to 1 metre (39 ins) high. The panicles are erect, contracted, with short-pedicelled spikelets which are blotched with dark purplish to brownish spots. The leaves are dark green, with short hairs on lower leaf-sheaths, and the ligules usually more than 5 millimetres (0·4 in.) long.

Most noticeable characteristics are the spirally twisted awns of the spikelets, the long ligules and the hairy leaf-sheaths.

Hairy Oat-grass is distributed throughout Europe. It has no special soil requirements, is drought-resistant and grows quite well on peaty soils. It occurs regularly in the grass on roadsides, meadows and in thickets. It has little value as fodder, for it has neither the quality nor the yield of cultivated forage grasses, but it has beautiful inflorescences and is an attractive feature in grasslands with its silvery, dark-brown-spotted spikelets and long, bent awns gleaming brightly in the sun. It is not good as a solitary subject but is of value in tall meadow grass-lands because of its minimal requirements and good growth.

a) vegetative part of the plant
b) section of culm with panicle
c) spikelet
d) detail of spikelet — grain with awned lemma and palea

192

a   c   d

b

Spring or **Common Wild Oat**

Avena fatua L.   Poaceae

The Common Wild Oat is a robust annual weed of arable land and waste places, growing and maturing at the same time as cultivated cereals. The panicles are broadly pyramidal with long, widely spreading branches bearing long-awned spikelets. The stout awns are black, bent and twisted, the seeds covered with rusty hairs at the base. The plant has very little foliage. The leaf-blades are finely rough, the ligules medium-sized and irregularly toothed.

It can be recognized by the large panicles with widely spreading, equally distributed branches bearing black-awned spikelets about 2 centimetres (0·8 in.) long.

The Common Wild Oat is a very abundant weed widely distributed throughout Europe which to a great extent has been successfully eradicated by modern methods of control. It generally ripens and seeds itself before cultivated cereals have been harvested, and so persists in the fields. It can be used for forage only until it begins to form ears.

The Common Wild Oat is closely related to the cultivated oats which differ from it in that they are very leafy, slow to harden and have seeds of high nutritional value. Planted for decorative purposes is *Avena glauca*, which is a compactly tufted species with beautiful blue-green leaves and large, attractive inflorescences. It may be used as a solitary subject in tall borders of the garden.

a) basal part of the plant
b) section of culm with panicle
c) detail of seed with awn

a   c   b

Spartina pectinata LINK
var. *aureomarginata*   Poaceae

Spartina pectinata is a drought-resistant perennial up to 2 metres (78 ins) high, spreading by stout rhizomes which in late May bear ascending culms with long leaves striped golden yellow and curving in large, elegant arches. In September it bears stout flower-topped culms often more than 3 metres (117 ins)high.

The main distinguishing factors of this variety are the gold-striped leaves, curving in a drooping arch with their sharp tips touching the ground.

Like most species of *Spartina*, it is a native of north-western America, where it grows on the margins of rivers. Some species are typical of the American prairies. It stands up well to both drought and damp, is frost-resistant and grows well even in moderate, partial shade. It is one of the most beautiful of the ornamental grasses. In botanical literature it is often listed as *S. michauxiana* var. *aureomarginata*.

Widespread in western Europe is the less decorative but extremely salt-loving *S. townsendii* (Townsend's Cord-grass), first discovered at the end of the eighteenth century on the shores of southern England. Of weaker habit and only about 50 centimetres (20 ins) high *S. maritima* (Cord-grass) is also widespread on the northern shores of the Adriatic. *Spartina* is of great value in improving the appearance of the coastal landscape and in building up natural shallows.

a) flowering panicle and part of the characteristic striped leaves
b) detail showing junction of leaf-blade and sheath

b   a

Porcupine Grass

Miscanthus sinensis (THUNB.) ANDERSS.   Poaceae
var. *variegatus*

This is a grass native to Japan and distinguished by its leaves patterned with yellow horizontal bands. It forms dense tufts of ascending culms with leaves in a flat, feather-like arrangement and stout rhizomes which overwinter and in Europe start into growth at the end of May. The leaves are green at first, with the yellow patterning gradually becoming more distinct until they resemble the spines of a porcupine — hence the common name of this grass in a number of different languages, Porcupine Grass. The yellow bands, more than 1 centimetre (0·4 in.) wide, are the chief distinguishing feature of this species. In late September, but more often in October, the culms grow to a height of 1·5 to 2 metres (58–78 ins) and bear panicles of attractive, reddish, silvery haired spikelets.

This and the Pampas Grass (*Cortaderia selloana*) are generally regarded as the most beautiful of all grasses. The loveliness of the glowing yellow, horizontal bands and arrangement of the leaves is matched by no other grass and it is no wonder that it is popular for ornamental purposes both as a solitary specimen and in groups.

Unlike *M. sinensis* var. *zebrinus* this variety is comparatively frost-resistant and in most parts of Europe does not need a protective cover in winter.

Another species of the genus worthy of note is *M. sacchariflorus*, which has spikelets which are practically awnless and is distinguished by its exceptional height. It is also known as *Imperata sacchariflora*.

a) vegetative part of the plant
b) winter habit of the plant

b   a

Pennisetum alopecuroides (L.) SPRENG. Poaceae

This is a robust, tufted perennial grass up to 60 centimetres (24 ins) high. In late summer it forms a great number of flower-bearing stalks terminated by cylindrical, brownish, spike-like panicles. The spikelets have short pedicels and long hairs at the base. The leaf-sheaths are wrapped around the stem; the leaf-blades are dark green, long, narrow and pointed, and the ligules are absent.

The chief characteristics to note are the long, contracted, spike-like panicles with long, brownish bristles. The tufts are bristle-like, about 70–80 centimetres (28–32 ins) across, the leaves spreading in all directions.

This grass was introduced into Europe from Australia as an ornamental. It does well in rich soils in sunny situations in parks and gardens, where it looks best as a solitary specimen. It is one of the most elegant of evergreen, ornamental grasses and very resistant to frost. In the autumn it is especially attractive with its numerous cylindrical, spike-like panicles. *Pennisetum* includes other species which are planted out as ornamentals, such as *P. villosum*, *P. ruppelii*, and others, native to Ethiopia, but these are annuals, about 70 centimetres (28 ins) high, flowering in August and usually finishing their life cycle with the onset of the first frost. These ornamental grasses are becoming increasingly popular and may be frequently found in European gardens.

a) part of the flowering plant
b) the same plant after the frost

a   b

Pampas Grass

Cortaderia selloana (SCHULT. et SCHULT. f.)   Poaceae
ASCHERS. et GRAEBN.

Pampas Grass is one of the most robust of drought-loving grasses, standing about 70 centimetres (28 ins) high, with long narrow leaves spreading regularly in all directions. In autumn it forms tall culms terminated by rich inflorescences of silvery white spikelets. The panicles are 45–75 centimetres (18–30 ins) long and the plant is often more than 2·5 metres (98 ins) high during the flowering period.

It is easily recognized by the large, dense tussocks with crowded, arching leaf-blades and in late summer the tall culms with large, silvery haired panicles.

Pampas Grass is a native of South America, originating from the pampas of Brazil. It enjoys hot, dry conditions and when grown in Europe must be provided with a protective covering in winter, such as a layer of dry leaves or bracken and evergreen branches. Except in the mildest areas, if left without protection it is often damaged or may even be killed by frost. For this reason it is not widely cultivated in Europe even though it has been known there since the eighteenth century, when it was first introduced to Ireland. It is a true gem of gardens and with its robust flowering tufts it is unrivalled as a solitary specimen. In the past decade new varieties have been produced, mostly of lower growth, with more gleamingly silver panicles and an earlier period of flowering.

In botanical literature this grass is also sometimes listed as *Gynerium argenteum*.

a) vegetative part of the plant
b) section of culm with large inflorescence
c) winter habit of the vegetative and flowering parts of the plant

Common Millet

Panicum miliaceum L.   Poaceae

Common Millet is a cultivated, thermophilous annual grass up to 1 metre (39 ins) high. In summer it bears stiff culms terminated by large, more or less contracted panicles drooping to one side. The spikelets are long-pedicelled, ovate, and unlike other grasses have three glumes. The leaves are broad and rough, the blades hairy. The ligules are short and may be hairy.

The chief distinguishing characteristics are the hairy leaf-sheaths and nodes and the heavy panicles drooping to one side and composed of awnless, rounded spikelets. The short-stalked spikelets and seeds are usually reddish, green or greyish. Millet is a native of Asia and is one of the cereal grasses that have been cultivated since the dawn of human civilization. In Europe it grows best in the drier southern regions but matures throughout the Continent.

Nowadays there are many different cultivated varieties. Common Millet occasionally becomes naturalized as a weed of waste places.

Some species of millet are important ornamental grasses. *P. virgatum* var. *strictum* forms handsome tufts up to 180 centimetres (71 ins) high which are very decorative in late summer. This species and *P. clandestinum,* forming dense tufts about 70 centimetres (28 ins) high, are natives of North America. Also frequently planted for decorative purposes is *P. capillare,* distinguished by the long, hair-like branches of the panicles spreading in all directions.

a) vegetative part of the plant
b) section of culm with panicles
c) detail of flowering spikelet

204

Bamboo

Bambusa metake FIEB. et NICHOLS   Poaceae

Bamboos are tall Oriental grasses with long, elliptical, evergreen leaves that grow to a length of 15–20 centimetres (6–8 ins) and are arranged in feather-like formation on the firm bamboo stems. Bamboos are very different from common grasses and include several different genera. They have woody, solid-jointed stems, flowers with three to six or more stamens and a fruit that may be a grain, but also a drupe or a berry. All bamboos are tropical or subtropical plants found chiefly in south-eastern Asia. Those that can be cultivated in Europe include *B. metake*, known also as *Pseudosasa japonica*. During the first years it requires a light protective covering in winter. The evergreen leaves are usually killed by frost and in spring the plant produces new shoots from the strong, creeping rhizomes. In mild winters or if provided with a protective covering of bracken the evergreen leaves survive.

This bamboo is a very handsome plant forming compact, circular, shrub-like tussocks and growing to a height of 3 metres (117 ins) in fertile soils. In Europe it generally does not flower.

Other bamboos suitable for growing in Europe include *B. japonica* (syn. *Arundinaria japonica*), which is extremely frost-resistant; *B. murielae* (syn. *Sinarundinaria murielae*), known as the Umbrella Bamboo; *B. nitida* (syn. *S. nitida*), a beautiful species with rich, delicate foliage; and *B. pygmaeae* (*Sasa pygmaea*), which is a dwarf species.

a) part of rhizome
b) leaves and stems
c) leaves and stems after severe frosts
c) detail of flowering spikelet

a   b   c   d

INDEX OF COMMON NAMES

INDEX OF LATIN NAMES